The Post-College Guide to Happiness

Bryan Cohen

DEDICATION

I dedicate this book to all of the people who at one time or another have put a smile on my face.

CONTENTS

Introduction   vii

1   Brainy Bliss   3

2   Money and Happiness   17

3   True Love and Contentment   39

4   Education and Joy   55

5   Gratification and Peace   69

6   Creativity and Lifelong Dreams   85

7   God and High Spirits   103

8   A Fully Rounded Life   119

Appendix 1: The 35 Exercises Simplified   123

Appendix 2: Happy Passive Income   127

Bibliography   129

About the Author   133

INTRODUCTION

If you heard a rumor about a foolproof, amazingly quick way to get rich, would you believe it? Would you be willing to spend your whole life on that pursuit, based solely on a rumor? If you're most people, you probably wouldn't. You'd be more likely to ignore it or gather some evidence on this "too good to be true" tip. Once you found out that it was full of crap, you'd probably push it to the back of your mind like the "secret to losing weight" or the "cream that makes you look younger with no side effects" or the "Swedish penis enlarger."

Why, then, are we willing to follow rumors of what is supposed to make us happy?

If you asked most people what would make them their happiest, they would probably say something like money, fame or power. They believe that having one or all of those three things would give them the freedom to do whatever they want. To them, that freedom equals happiness. I mean, it's obvious, right? After they did all those studies about the extremely happy lives of the rich, famous and powerful. At least, I think they did some studies about that, didn't they? Who are *they*, anyway? What am I subtly hinting at?

I'm saying that happiness as a result of money and position is as much of a rumor as the success stories of the "Swedish penis enlarger."

If happiness doesn't come from these sources, it must be present in another aspects of life, like family, career, love, sex, food or something else, right? Sure, some of those things can make you feel good every so often, but with all the broken families, workaholics, divorces, addicts and morbidly overweight people out there, no one thing functions as a 100 percent solution. Still, most people in the world share the assumption that one of the above items will make them truly happy.

When I was growing up, my parents often told me that they didn't care what I did with my life as long as it made me happy. Well then how come there doesn't seem to be a clear answer of how to *be* happy?

Through four years of immediate gratification and finding out what I wanted to do with my life, I didn't learn the answer to that question during my enjoyable stay in college. The most frequently used answer to the question was along the lines of "you'll have fun in school and then you'll have to work hard the rest of your life to get the stuff and people you want."

That is an awful answer. That's like going into a doctor's office for a leg cramp and her saying, "I can give you this prescription to feel better for a while, but it's going to hurt like hell until you die." There had to be someone with a better answer.

I went searching. I listened to podcasts, I read books and I trolled through websites. There would be an article here or a spot-on quote there but there was never a fully fleshed-out theory. And then I found Marci.

No, Marci was not the pixy free-spirited love of my life resembling Natalie Portman's character from *Garden State* who made me forget about this silly quest for happiness. She was an author who wrote the book *Happy for No Reason* (along with co-writer Carol Kline), which gave me my "aha moment" for understanding happiness. Marci Shimoff's book convinced me that happiness was attainable. Her book was mostly geared toward a self-helpy, middle-aged crowd, which she'd written for in her other books like *Chicken Soup for the Woman's Soul* and *Love for No Reason*.

While I loved the book, I couldn't help but think that most people my age wouldn't pick up a book like that in a million years. And if that were true, it could decades before my favorite peers in the world would start going the right direction when it came to happiness.

This saddened me (not quite as much as FOX cancelling "Firefly" did, but pretty close), and I decided to do something about it. I wanted to write a guide to happiness for people who have recently graduated from college and who are looking to make a name for themselves. I wanted to stop these rumors of what *might* bring on happiness and start telling the world the truth.

As many of us try to slip into a world of digital oblivion, with 24/7 staring at our jumbo-sized iDevices with apps that can do anything and everything while deadening our emotions, I hope that this book can help people starting out in the "real world" to head toward happiness instead of drifting in the wind and hoping for the best.

The Lucky Ones

I realize that this book isn't for everyone. There are some people who are fortunate enough to have figured out happiness all on their own. These people wake up each morning with a smile and go to bed the exact same way. They embark on their daily source (or sources) of income with fervor and they treat their loved ones with respect, an open heart and an open mind. If you are one of these people, I applaud you and I aspire to be as completely happy as you some day.

Several years out of school, I was more or less your opposite. A lot of other folks would say the same. I liked going to work sometimes, but most of the time I wished I could be anywhere else. I avoided looking at my bank account. I wasn't pleased with my social life. I didn't have a great relationship with my closest loved ones. There were many aspects of my existence that could easily be classified as unhappy. This is a book for those of you who have felt the same at some point.

I don't think that happiness should simply come by chance or by genetics. I believe that we should all be the lucky ones. Everyone should be able to work a satisfying job. We should all be able to come home and take care of our loved ones and feel love in return. We deserve to be happy most, if not all, of the time. Happiness should not just be an occasional moment that is bordered on each side by misery and stoicism. It should be something we all aspire to.

A Happy Life

In this book, I have broken down the major sources of post-college unhappiness into seven categories. I've tried to include nearly every aspect of life in these pages, from that paying-the-bills job to the unfulfilling game-playing on your iDevice. Here is how I've set up the book.

Chapter 1: Brainy Bliss

If you have the life you want and you can't seem to find happiness, there's a good chance the issue is located upstairs. Tweaking a few mental issues may help you get in the right direction.

Chapter 2: Money and Happiness

Many college students and students of the world get into their line of work because they think it will lead to money, fame and joy. They eventually realize that the best things in life are free, such as a set of worthy goals that make you feel fulfilled with the work you put in every day.

Chapter 3: True Love and Contentment

There's nothing quite like finding someone you love and want to spend the rest of your life with. The next trick is making sure your happiness doesn't rely completely on someone else, which can be accomplished by learning to love yourself and embracing empathy.

Chapter 4: Education and Joy

Extending education past college and through various master's and doctorate programs has its advantages. Just make sure you aren't using these degrees to avoid learning about yourself and the world around you.

Chapter 5: Gratification and Peace

As technology advances and society becomes more laid back, it's easy to be entertained from the beginning of the day until the lights go out. Taking time to embrace nothingness every once in a while, however, may make regular life as exciting as that new fangled toy.

Chapter 6: Creativity and Lifelong Dreams

Many people in the artistic, creative and theatrical world have immense dreams of "making it" in a tough field. Those who have trouble tend to meet setbacks with drinking, drugs and other deadening activities. Embrace your dreams with visualization to make them more attainable and to keep yourself vibrant.

Chapter 7: God and High Spirits

A major part of happiness is to have a distinct spiritual aspect of your life. Using that belief to trample the beliefs of others is not likely to breed joy in your world. Ask the spiritual world for a peaceful and prosperous life and it shall be given.

Chapter 8: A Fully Rounded Life

Putting all the ducks in a row from your brain to your beliefs can set you on the path to a lifetime of happiness.

But I Want It

Upon editing the book, my super heroine editor Ashley Daoust came up with a strong point. When I say phrases like "I/you/we deserve to be happy" does that include jerks who say mean things to people to get a buzz, push old ladies down the stairs for the heck of it and at the end of the day go to bed with a smile on their faces? Here's the thing about happiness: it goes hand in hand with character. Many of the exercises in this book discuss ways to bring you closer to your family, friends, spirituality and even yourself. My belief is that when you start making those parts of your life more important, the nasty things you do like skipping out on your problems to feel good or ditching your loving partner to sleep with some floozy won't be as important to you anymore. You'll realize that a big part of happiness is about being a good person, not just a person who gets everything he or she wants.

Higher Education

I realize that this book has "college" in the title, but I certainly don't mean it to be only for students who have just graduated from college. I know plenty of successful and happy people who chose to forego college. I also don't want people to think that this is only a book for grads, graduate students and those who haven't attached themselves to a spouse or a mortgage yet. I learned a lot from reading books and listening to audio tracks that were geared toward the middle-aged self-development crowd. In contrast, I think that people of all ages could get a kick in the pants out of this book, even though it points to the post-college aged crowd a bit.

I thought that I had everything figured out when I graduated from college. Many college graduates think the same way. I was surprised to find out that despite learning to be more outspoken, impulsive and fun-loving during my higher education years, it was some of my traits I had in high school that pulled me toward finding happiness. In high school, I adopted the philosophy to enjoy at least one aspect about every class I took and to concentrate fully on that thing. While, I'll admit, concentrating on the attractive Israeli girl in my Geometry class didn't keep my grades very high, the way of thinking was a much-needed boost to my happiness during my awkward adolescent years. This experience proved to me that no matter how young I was or no matter how young a source of advice is, good advice is good advice, period. Don't assume that your purveyor of wisdom needs to be some stuffy doctorate from Harvard, because it might be a 15-year-old kid, a 30-year-old author or even middle-aged parent with flashes of brilliance.

Learning is mandatory for the first 18 years of your life. After that, some take on an extra four or more years to lock into a trade or career. The true secret of happiness, as I'll lay out in the following 10,000 pages (just kidding, it's less than 200), is a matter of learning more about yourself and the world as your life moves forward. If you shut yourself off to learning and practicing the art of happiness, you'll miss out on one of the more important lessons of life.

Happiness is not a rich or a poor thing. It's not something given solely to people who are genetically gifted or who are born in a certain part of the world. Happiness is something earned day in and day out. It is something practiced and cultivated like any other skill. It must be nurtured, manipulated and sculpted until you wake up one morning with a silly grin and realize that you're in the thick of it. Bliss.

I hope you thoroughly enjoy the book.

Sincerely,
Bryan Cohen
Author of *The Post-College Guide to Happiness*

Bryan Cohen

A NOTE ON THE HAPPINESS WORKOUTS

Since many people go to a gym (or at least belong to a gym), I figured I'd put some happiness action plans in the form of workouts at the end of each chapter. Most of the chapters have the task of convincing you that happiness is attainable in the different areas of your life. If you are a "skip to the action" kind of person, you could always go to the end of every chapter and use the workouts right away. While I've paired specific exercises with targeted discussions of happiness, feel free to mix and match the exercises as you see fit. Look at it as cross-training to improve your overall levels of happy fitness.

In the workouts, I suggest setting aside half an hour for each training session. If you have less time, cut down the exercises to fit your needs. If you have more time, there's no harm in lengthening the session or adding workouts from other chapters. Including a happiness workout alongside your typical cardiovascular or strength training can leave you feeling fit inside and out. Keep both sets up and it won't take long for the people around you to notice. Including yourself!

CHAPTER 1: BRAINY BLISS

I've read many interesting and informative articles about happiness as part of my research for this project and for my own personal development. The most important article I read, however, had nothing to do with happiness but may have had the largest impact on my research and my structure of this book. It made me realize that the practice of happiness wasn't something for an enlightened few but for everybody on the planet. Why is this possible? Why do all people, optimistic or pessimistic, old or young, male or female, Christmas or Festivus, have the opportunity to become happier people? Because all of us have a brain.

In the field of neurology, which deals with the brain and the nervous system, the belief was that once your brain grew to full size in adolescence, it was more or less fixed. When you stopped learning languages and arithmetic in school, your brain was thought to be unlikely to change much for the rest of your life. In fact, it was also believed that parts of your brain would just sort of shut off slowly but surely until your dying day with no chance of reprieve. If a part of your noggin was lost, it was lost for good. This supposed immutability led most people to believe that if they were "angry people" or "stubborn people" or "constipated people" that it was the brain they were born with and there wasn't much changing it.

Just as scientists changed their opinions about smoking being good for you and Pluto being a planet, they also determined that the brain became far from fixed. It turns out that if you're an "angry person" or a "stubborn person" you actually *can* change. The brain is made up of neural pathways that electrical currents run through. Like a newly paved road, the neural pathways are most effective in an area of the brain you use frequently. If you are a baker, the neural pathways around using your hands and smelling and tasting food are well-maintained and contain few potholes. The pathways around the parts of the brain you don't use? Think of those as an old, bumpy country road that takes a while to get over. If the baker doesn't do much math and tries to help his tenth grade daughter with a math problem, he can almost feel his brain struggling to get through his unused neural pathways. I'm sure most people have felt the same sensation when trying to solve a problem in an unfamiliar area.

The new discovery in neurology, though, is that if you work on a certain area of the brain, no matter how old you are, you can strengthen those neural pathways. If you take up baking or the violin or *compassion* later in life, you can alter your brain to fit what you want it to be and do. In short, if you are an unhappy person for no discernible reason, you can strengthen your neural pathways to optimism, friendship, joy, peace and other aspects of life associated with happiness.

Not surprisingly, it can take societal beliefs a long time to catch up to science. Despite this adaptable brain, people still think that if they've been a certain way for their entire lives that they are doomed to stay that way. The good news for you is that, since you've picked up this book, you will be exposed to some mental happiness exercises that can start to get you back on the right track.

What Is Mental Unhappiness?

Truth be told, every type of unhappiness has a little bit of mental unhappiness thrown in for bad measure. Straight up mental unhappiness comes from generally having your life put together but still feeling unhappy at the end of the day. Obviously, there are stresses of daily life and there are negative things that can happen to you throughout the day. These things are unavoidable unless you decide to shun life and live in a tree or a cave in some new country. The true measure of whether or not you are happy comes when you are at neutral.

Examine the space between the negative and positive things that happen to you in life. Maybe your neutral time comes when you're walking to the train for work before you start thinking about your to-do list. Maybe it happens the second before you turn on the television to start zoning out for the night. Perhaps it occurs the few minutes before you fall asleep. If you ask yourself the question, "Am I happy right at this moment?" and the answer is no, then you may require a routine series of happiness workouts.

A note here for those who have been diagnosed with clinical depression: Mental unhappiness is more like the blues, occasionally feeling down but not feeling down for weeks or months at a time. Clinical depression is not the same thing as mental unhappiness. It is a medical condition that can be best treated by a trained physician. If you find that you are extremely unhappy all the time and that even the good things that happen to you don't tend to snap you out of it, you should speak with your doctor.

What Do You Deserve?

As far as I can figure it, there are two kinds of people who are mentally unhappy. There are those who have been mildly to moderately unhappy for their entire lives for no apparent reason. They lead a generally fair-to-middling sort of life and have a decent job, a loving family and a dog named Scruff, but for some reason they cannot seem to put a smile on their faces for too long. The other type of mental unhappiness comes from an unfortunate place. It happens to people who think they *deserve* to be unhappy.

I'll admit that for a long time I was in this unhappy boat. I was a nice kid, growing up. I liked helping people and hanging with my friends and giving advice to people who were having a tough time. I thought of myself as a good person, but I could never put my finger on what I needed to do to be happy. I figured that perhaps I'd done something gravely wrong during my lifetime or that my fate was to be unhappy.

Let's imagine a little scenario here. Say that you are a fun-loving athlete who is obsessed with baseball. You eat, sleep and live baseball from the time the sun comes up until they turn out the lights at your favorite playing field. Your hope is to become a wildly successful professional player. You do all the right workouts and learn from the best coaches possible. There's only one problem. Almost every time you go out to play, rain comes pouring down like crazy. You want to play baseball every second of the day, but almost like clockwork, when you go out to play it starts to rain.

Some people might assume that the rain is their fault. It's some kind of cosmic message that baseball is not the sport for them.

Now what if I told you that you lived in Seattle, Washington, and that it rains all the time there? Obviously the rain is not your fault, it's just the circumstances you happen to be in, which are beyond your control.

If you've had a life with some misfortune and general unhappiness, you may believe that this is simply the way the world works. In reality, most hardships you endure are probably the result of circumstances beyond your control. Perhaps you were born with a less upbeat personality than your friends and in comparison you seem unhappy. Maybe your family was tough on you and made you feel like you weren't worth being joyful. There are all sorts of circumstance that can play into your current level of happiness and your belief of how deserving a person you are. Nobody deserves to be unhappy, and it is your right to go out there and play ball!

A Mental Rut

We tend to laugh when we see things like our dog circling around an equal number of times to sit down on a couch or when a cat starts scratching rhythmically on a fluffy blanket. These things are amusing because it almost seems like the animal can't help but follow the same routine that has been bred into them. Of course, we're way different from dogs and cats, right? I'm sure they don't laugh at our routines of getting pissy in the morning, plopping down in front of the television and zoning out and grumbling about our issues at work with our partner.

If we are going to push past our habits of mental unhappiness, we need to be willing to shake things up a little bit. I've seen plenty of people in action who have a daily negative routine that couldn't help but cause them a bit of unhappiness. I've seen others who know that a routine is bringing them down but they do nothing to change it. The reason they don't change it is that it's easier to stay the same. It takes a special kind of effort to move your life in a different direction and some people would rather stay comfortably unhappy. Let's just say, this is not a book for those people.

If it's possible to change your brain, that means it's possible to change your negative habits. But we don't have to change them all at once. Getting your brain happy is not a process that happens overnight and it's always best to make small changes at first. For instance, during my reading about personal development and happiness, I started paying attention to the little things I was doing that may have been throwing me off in the quest for a better life. I had the problem of getting angry about something that didn't go my way and then throwing myself a little pity party. Despite my best efforts to bring my most positive self to the front, I was having a difficult time stopping the pity parties, until I realized what I was doing habitually during these mini internal outbursts (would you call those inbursts?). I was holding my breath. Every time I let my negative emotions build up, I was holding in my breath.

As best as I could figure it, I must have gotten some kind of rush from these bursts of negativity, and there was a part of me that actually liked them. By holding my breath in, it was almost like keeping the emotions in so they could bounce around me for a while before I let them out. I began to practice breathing deeply every time I could feel some negativity creeping in. Even making this small change was difficult, but when I created a new pathway between negativity and breathing deeply, I noticed fewer and fewer pity parties. It turned out that a little extra oxygen made a big difference as far as my mental routine was concerned.

What are some of the things you do that tend to set aside added negativity? Here are a few questions that you can ask yourself:

- Do you feel a little bit worse about your situation when you post about it on Facebook or Twitter?
- Do you have a common activity you do when you get mad that riles you up even more, like stomping your feet, clenching your fists or grinding your teeth?
- Is there a certain conversation topic you frequently engage in that makes you upset?
- Are there any objects in your home that only bring you sad memories?
- Is there something you do everyday like eating an extra muffin that you wish you could take back but you keep doing it over and over again?

A rut is a path that you keep walking continuously until there is literally a groove or a hole where you are standing. If you change the path, you eventually exit the rut. You don't have to change everything at once if you want to be a happier person. Make small changes of this nature throughout the next few weeks and months and you'll notice major changes in your emotions.

Stereotyping Optimists

Optimists tend to get a bit of a bad rap. When some people think of an optimist, they imagine a Mr. Magoo type who bumbles around ignoring all the depressing things in the world and talks about how amazing life is. They think of optimists as idiots with big goofy grins and a complete lack of intelligence. Personally, that seems like a bit of a, elementary school coping method to me. Like how you don't have a cool pair of shoes, so "that brand of shoes is stupid!" I think it's time to stop discriminating against the optimists.

I'm a comedian who happens to be an optimist (I feel like I'm in one of those "I'm a Mormon" commercials). If you've watched comedy, well, ever, you've probably noticed that many jokes rely on complaining, negativity and heartache. The old Woody Allen line of "Tragedy plus time equals comedy" has certainly been exhibited in most stand-up comedy and situational comedies I've watched throughout my life. Correct use of the formula tends to work quite well, but I don't believe it's the only way. Comedy can be about truth, intelligent observations and sharing experiences with people. I learned to do comedy while dispensing with nearly all the negativity that tends to crop up in most acts, but it wasn't easy. It took a lot of work, internally and externally.

Life is a lot like comedy in that optimism is the more difficult choice. You have to push yourself harder and keep yourself from picking the easier choice of complaining or whining about something in your life. It's way easier to be pissed off about something than it is to be grateful for the things you already have. Being cynical and seeing the rough stuff in the world is so much simpler than it is to keep your mood and the mood of the people around you lofty. Do you truly want to be happy? Then get ready to be part of the minority. Be prepared to put in the time and effort you will require to change yourself from a pessimist into an optimist.

Workout for Brainy Bliss

Exercise #1: Mental Aerobics

In the book *Keep Your Brain Alive*, authors Lawrence C. Katz, Ph.D., and Manning Rubin describe 83 exercises that stimulate your brain and foster the creation of new mental pathways, such as the new road between your thoughts and optimism. In order to make sure that your brain is primed for accepting these novel happiness blueprints, it's worth doing a few of these interesting and innovative mental exercises. While I won't go into all 83 exercises here, I will give a few examples and the general concept of mental aerobics, which the authors refer to as "neurobics."

The basic idea behind mental aerobics is that your brain is used to certain patterns in relation to your five senses and your memory. You are used to grabbing your keys out of your left pocket and then transferring them to your right hand to open your front door. You always take the same roads when you're driving home from work. Every Sunday you smell the aroma of pancakes wafting in from the kitchen. By confusing your brain with new stimuli mixed in with the old stimuli, your brain generates the chemicals needed to build new roads.

Here are a few ideas of mental aerobics to start your brainy bliss workout plan:

- Move your phone and keys to the opposite pocket of your pants
- Take a shower with your eyes closed
- Walk down several streets you've never taken and find your way back home
- Light a scented candle when you wake up in the morning
- Teach yourself to write with your opposite hand

The key with these exercises (and any that you come up with on your own) is to test them out for at least a couple of weeks, because it takes your brain a little bit of time to start forming the new pathways.

At first, doing these activities may feel like learning to walk again, because they will be completely unfamiliar to your brain. After a little while, you'll feel more comfortable doing them and your brain will be ready to accept the positive changes you want to foist upon it.

Exercise #2: I Spy – Appreciation Edition

In the book *Ask and It Is Given,* Esther and Jerry Hicks discuss an exercise called "The Rampage of Appreciation," which is essentially a mix of the game "I Spy" with a healthy dose of optimism. When you are having issues with feeling happy in your otherwise pleasant life, you are used to having a great deal of negative thoughts. Playing this game with yourself can help train you to think more positively about the people and things around you.

Take a walk around your house, apartment or neighborhood and every so often focus on an object. Start listing the reasons you appreciate that object (either mentally or on paper). For instance, you might see a tree and say to yourself, "I appreciate this tree. It absorbs pollution so I don't have to breathe it and it provides me with oxygen. It gives the birds a place to hang out and aesthetically it's a nice departure from the city streets. I'm glad this tree is here." You get the idea. I realize that it's a little hokey, but I'll take a lifetime of hokey over unexplained sadness any day.

Here are a few ideas of objects and people you can try out the exercise on:

- Your car, your bike or the bus you take
- The sky, the clouds or the sun
- A local park, playground or movie theater
- Your television, DVD collection and computer
- Your parents, friends and favorite barista

You may be inclined to include things like "But, I don't like when it does this," adding negativity to an otherwise positive thing. I realize that this might happen at first when your cynicism tries to take over. Hold yourself to doing the exercise as described, because over time, this exercise as-is can make a major difference in how you look at the world.

Exercise #3: The Sedona Method®

I first found out about The Sedona Method® through Marci Shimoff's *Happy for No Reason*. The method was created in 1952 by a man named Lester Levenson. He had been diagnosed with a fatal health condition at the age of 40 and was sent home to live his final days. After creating a methodology for releasing all his negative thoughts and feelings over the course of three months, his body was completely healed and he lived for another 40 years. This is another exercise that some could see as hippy-dippy, but I've found it to be extremely helpful during my most difficult days on my journey to happiness.

The Sedona Method® is predicated on the belief that your feelings are not part of you. While we might say things like "I am angry" or "I am scared," it doesn't actually mean that these emotions take us over and become who we are. Marci learned the method from Levenson's protégé, Hale Dwoskin, who continues to teach the principles of the exercise today. Dwoskin described the concept behind the method as such: take a pen in your hand and imagine that the pen represents your thoughts and your feelings while your hand represents your awareness. Roll the pen around on the palm of your hand. The pen (your feelings and thoughts) are not a part of your hand (your awareness). Turn your hand over and drop the pen. Using the proper method, it is possible to let go of those feelings as easily as you were able to drop the pen.

Here's how the method works:
1. Ask yourself the question, "Could I let this feeling go?"
2. Answer the question in your head or out loud.
3. Then ask the question, "Would I let it go?"
4. Once again, answer the question.
5. Then ask, "When?"
6. Answer it.

The first time I read about the method, I said to myself, "That's it?" Then I tried it. Even though my answers to the question the first go around were "no," "no" and "are you kidding me?" I inexplicably felt better. Simply by asking these questions, my mind starting wondering if I could, in fact, let these negative thoughts out of my pesky head. I've gotten a lot of wonderful mileage out of this exercise and I can attest to its effectiveness at dispensing negativity and making room for positive thoughts.

Exercise #4: Optimism Journal

In Martin E.P. Seligman, Ph.D.'s book *Learned Optimism*, Seligman discusses the differences between pessimists and optimists, and it really comes down to something called explanatory style. He talks about the ABCs, which stand for moments of adversity, followed by beliefs and, lastly, consequences. Seligman gives a great example of a person going off her diet one night and then giving up on the entire endeavor because it's "ruined" (which has happened to me personally on more than one occasion). The *adversity* in this situation is that the woman has gone off of the diet. She *believes* that her diet is ruined and the *consequence* is that she eats a hefty brownie dessert and quits.

Going off a diet for one night, getting a scratch on your car, missing the payment on a credit card or stubbing your toe is not the end of the world. People with a positive explanatory style are able to write these off as random events that are out of their control in an otherwise happy life. As Dr. Richard Carlson says in his book of the same name, "Don't sweat the small stuff – and it's all small stuff." Those with a negative explanatory style will bitch and moan and whine about the tiniest things and act like Chicken Little, proclaiming the world to be.

For those looking to convert from pessimist to optimist, Seligman suggests taking down the ABCs of a few recent situations and thinking about how you could have changed your beliefs to alter the scenario's consequences. I think you should take it one step further.

In the first week of your optimism journal (which can be as simple as a notepad or a word processor document), write down five instances of adversity, belief and consequence from the past week or month in which you were not optimistic. Write down how you could have acted differently to exhibit more optimism. In the second week, make an active effort to be optimistic. Since nobody is perfect, write down two instances in which you were successful in your optimism and two in which you were pessimistic at the end of the week. Keep this up until you can't think of any instances of pessimism and then detail your optimistic week with another set of ABCs.

Exercise #5: A New Project

Your brainy bliss workout plan includes some mental gymnastics to get your brain ready to change, a way to look more positively at the things around you, a procedure to let go of your persistent negativity and a method for training yourself to be more optimistic in situations. Now we will endeavor to take on a new project that will both stimulate your brain *and* get you out of your mental rut.

List five things that you want to do that you've never been able to get up the energy or the motivation to accomplish.

Here are some examples of new projects you could take on:

- Learning a new language
- Shooting a short film about your neighborhood
- Study a new dance with your partner or friends
- Joining a rock-climbing club
- Taking up cooking, sewing, painting, sculpting, yoga, etc.

Making a new project a part of your life has a dual-benefit. When you give your brain something new to think about or a new movement (in the case of dancing, climbing, yoga, etc.) you are stimulating your brain to create new pathways, just like you did with mental aerobics. In addition, you are giving yourself something fresh and exciting to do, which can be wonderful to look forward to at the end of a tough day. I've been a little less specific with this exercise because a new project can really take any form, but that doesn't mean you should take it less seriously. It is the ingredient that brings the dish together, as they say.

The Plan

Here is a sample weekly plan that you can use to deploy your exercises. Feel free to use it exactly as is or to change it to fit your schedule and available time and energy.

Monday: Do some Mental Aerobics in the morning, followed by work on your Optimism Journal. In the evening, brainstorm on your New Project.

Tuesday: Try out I Spy – Appreciation Edition in the morning to give yourself an optimistic outlook throughout the day and use the Sedona Method® if you slip into pessimism.

Wednesday: Take some action on your New Project, like taking a class or having a study session.

Thursday: Repeat Monday's morning plan with an evening dose of the Sedona Method®.

Friday: Repeat Tuesday's plan with some additional brainstorming on your New Project.

Saturday and Sunday: Take the weekend off or make up for anything you didn't get to during the week.

Final Thoughts

I hope that I've convinced you that even if you've always felt a little bit short of happy, you can achieve that state with a few minor alterations. While changing your brain to make yourself a healthier and more joyful person isn't the latest rage yet, I think in the next few decades we'll be seeing more and more of it. You may as well be one of the first to get a jump on it! It's not easy teaching your brain new tricks, but the sheer fact that it's possible and that happiness is in reach can act as enough of a goal to keep you on the straight and narrow, if you let it.

CHAPTER 2: MONEY AND HAPPINESS

The belief that more money on its own would definitely lead to an increased level of happiness is sort of strange to me. I would assume that people might get this opinion from movies and other pop culture, but most wealthy people in fiction are portrayed as total dicks. In addition, there are phrases like "money can't buy happiness" that have been used so often as to become cliché. Lastly, there have been countless tales of the rich and famous becoming thoroughly unhappy and turning to addictions and suicide attempts to alleviate their unhappiness. Despite all of this, most of the people in the world believe that if they had more money, they would be bubbling over with happiness.

One of the reasons this belief has been perpetuated is that we associate being happy with doing fun stuff. If you are rich, you are more likely to be able to do as many entertaining things as possible. I don't dispute that when I'm out playing Ultimate Frisbee or lounging on the beach, I feel incredibly good. Putting your worries on hold for a minute and taking in a show or a movie is great. It makes sense that if you can continue to put your problems on the back burner and take in as many awesome events as possible that you would be happier in general. The issue is that having fun and being happy are not the same thing.

Let me say that again: having fun and being happy are not the same thing.

I once heard a quote along the lines of "The person you love isn't necessarily who you want to spend Friday night with, but who you want to spend all day Saturday with." Happiness is the same sort of thing. You want to have a great time when you're out on the town and have as much fun as possible. When you're back at home the next day and you're surrounded by the everyday tasks of life, you want to feel good even when you're not having fun. That's what happiness is. It's a sense of love and joy that fills your existence between the moments of hardship and enjoying yourself. It's what Marci Shimoff refers to as "happy for no reason."

Let's imagine another scenario here. Let's say that you went to college (and perhaps graduate school) in hopes of getting a high paying career like in a legal or business field. Along the way you've determined that you will not be truly happy until you become "successful." Success, in your mind, is nothing less than having the best stuff possible, being able to take the most amazing vacations and having your own corner office in the high-rise building of a prestigious company. Now, if there are millions of people in the world who believe they won't be happy without this end result and there are only a thousand or so positions available, this leads to a whole lot of perceived unhappiness, right? Doesn't seem quite right to me. Now let's suppose that you are one of the thousand fortunate souls who actually gets one of the positions. Now imagine that you've earned the office, taken the vacations and bought all of the best things that money can buy, but it still feels sort of unfulfilling.

What's the next step in such a scenario? For many people, even with a high income and a fantastic job, it's buying more things and more extravagant vacations. It's a game of "keeping up with the Joneses" which can lead to a lot of debt and a miniscule amount of gratification. Say you are one of the thousand people with the fabulous job, and you're laid off during a recession. If you've been "playing the game," you might be completely screwed! After twenty years of working and buying, you end up back at square one, no happier than you were when you started. This happened to tens of thousands of people during the recent financial troubles of 2008 to 2011, and it led to foreclosure and bankruptcy. It occurred, in part, because people believed that more money would bring them increased happiness, but it really only led to mo' problems.

What Do You Really Want?

What is it about having stuff and boatloads of money that is so appealing? Do we really want a ridiculous mansion that could fit 40 people inside when we have a family of four? Do we need a boat, a motorcycle and a classic car when losing our job would mean we'd have to quickly sell them? Do we need to shop at the premium grocery store for freshly prepared organic food when we could spend a little extra time preparing it ourselves for half the price? What do we really want here?

I'm not sure if I have the answers to all of these questions. I think that some of it has to do with advertising and having the message beamed into our heads that we are somehow worse off without the best detergent, clothes, houses, phones and kids. Some of it has to do with a desire to somehow "win" life by getting all the most amazing stuff possible. Part of it has to do with this ridiculous sense that if we have more stuff it will equate into a permanent emotional boost. Like one dollar spent equals one unit of joy or something like that. Many of us have set a goal for ourselves to be rich, materialistic consumers.

I think it's time for us to make a new set of goals.

While a lot of people have goals to accomplish at work, goals to accomplish at home or goals that they've picked up along the way from society, most people in the "real world" don't have that many goals of their own. This is surprising. Especially since one of the few pleasures employees tend to get from a workplace is finishing a major project. It leaves them feeling accomplished and validated. The same thing goes at home when completing a renovation or a paint job. It feels good to get something done. Imagine if you focused on an objective that was loftier and more personal.

In the book *The Official Guide to Success*, motivator Tom Hopkins says, "Jonas Salk's great aim wasn't to become head of the lab so he could qualify for a pension. He set his sights on conquering polio."

Most of us are simply trying to get through the day as a goal. We pray that we can somehow make it to the next break without having to do much work and then we hope for the same thing after lunch. When we head home, we think to ourselves, "mission accomplished," when in fact it really wasn't much of a mission at all. We do the same thing the next day out of habit and before you know it, it's been five years or a decade. If you like your job and feel that you're doing the work you were meant to do there, that's great to hear and I wish you the best. If you despise your job and talk smack about it the moment you leave until the second you return, we have an issue.

You should love what you do, even if you don't like parts of it. If you don't even *like* what you do, of course you're unhappy. Spending a good chunk of your time involved in a task that you don't find stimulating, satisfying or interesting can be a major bummer. What did I do when I realized that I was in a job that was getting me nowhere fast in my mid-twenties? I quit.

I took personal development guru Steve Pavlina's words to heart: "Getting a job is like enrolling in a human domestication program. You learn how to be a good pet. Look around you. Really look. What do you see? Are these the surroundings of a free human being? Or are you living in a cage for unconscious animals? Have you fallen in love with the color beige?"

Now, what happened as soon as I leapt from employment to working for myself, looking for a calling that would make me happy and fulfilled? I struggled. I struggled mightily. But I was able to set new goals for myself, such as finding a new line of work that would allow me to reach more people as part of my newfound purpose. I started writing for people who were struggling to get their voices heard through the printed and digital worlds. I wanted those who were afraid to write and afraid to achieve their creative goals to push past their fears and to get their words onto the page.

It was a goal that much more closely aligned with what I wanted to do, and while it took a couple of years, I eventually doubled my previous income with no ceiling in sight of what I could earn.

Now before you go running off (and running off at the mouth to your boss), I'm not saying that you should go and quit your job right away. You may be in a financial situation where you have to have a new job lined up so that you don't miss out on a precious paycheck. This might behoove you to stay in your unhappy job until you secure something more up your alley. You may also be in a high-paying job that you don't like and the field you do enjoy is much lower paying. This might require you to save up some money in your current job before you are able to move on. This poses the question, how can I enjoy myself more in my current job?

There are a few things you can do. The first step is to stop complaining about and discussing the negative aspects of your job with your friends, family and co-workers. Have you ever had a nurse or doctor tell you that something they were about to do was going to hurt? Did you get twitchy or nervous? How about when they just did it without warning like ripping a bandage clean off? Which was a better experience?

Now imagine that you had an awful task to accomplish at work. You complain to your cubicle mate about how little you want to do this unenviable assignment. At lunch, you and your co-workers continue to talk about this tortuous upcoming issue. When you speak with your partner, the first thing you do is whine about the horrible pain you are about to endure. After all of that, when you finally get up to doing the task, it's like walking over a bed of hot coals. What if you had dispensed with all of the negativity and worked on the task without any buildup? It wouldn't be nearly as bad as you're making it out to be. Rip the bandage off and keep trucking along.

Secondly, start looking for the aspects of the job that you actually enjoy. They might be tough to find at first, but perhaps you look forward to seeing your co-workers. Maybe there is a particular boss that you appreciate having as a mentor. There might even be a presentation that you have a good time delivering. The positive parts of a job will differ from profession to profession, but they are present no matter what you do. Make a list of them and whenever your friends and co-workers try to goad you into talking about the negative traits, either think about or discuss the things that you like about working there.

Lastly, try to be the most effective employee on the face of the planet. Combine a dash of enthusiasm, two parts optimism and a sprig of helpfulness and make an effort to become more successful at your job. If you have to be a cog in the wheel, be the best damn cog the company has.

If you take these steps of eliminating negativity, increasing gratitude and becoming a more valuable employee, you will start to feel more empowered and you may even create new opportunities for yourself at your current job. It's often the most positive, grateful, enthusiastic people that get raises and the attention of their higher-ups. Why not put yourself in that category to increase your overall happiness?

The Secret to Loving the Work You Do: Goals

In our lives, we've set more than a few goals for ourselves. Whether it was asking out that cute girl or boy to the prom or finishing that tough level in Final Fantasy VII, we determined that the goal was worth putting in the time to achieve. Unfortunately, a lot of people stop setting goals after high school and college and sort of "go with the flow" for the rest of their lives. I used to think this laissez-faire approach was the key to happiness. I was wrong.

If you never set goals for yourself, you will have a tough time ever feeling fulfilled. Even if you generally know what you want, if you never take the time to write your goals down, you are much less likely to achieve them.

Becoming an eternally positive and reliable employee is great, and leaving your job to find work that you love to do is an equally awesome choice. In my opinion, however, the true key to being happy in your career is not a matter of money or position, it's a matter of setting amazing goals for yourself and working toward their achievement.

There are tons of books out there about goal setting and I suggest you read as many of them as you can get your hands on. The more you learn about setting great goals, the better you will be at it. One of my favorite books about goal setting is called *See You at the Top* by the amazingly named Zig Ziglar. In his book he sets out a seven-step plan for setting goals for yourself. Here they are, in a particular order.

Step 1: State the Goal

Has this ever happened to you? Over the course of a week, several different people have asked you different variations on the question, "What is your main goal?" Maybe they've asked, "What is your ambition?" or "What do you want to do with your life?" or even "Where do you see yourself in 10 years?" To answer the questions you use the repeat the words "sorta" or "kinda" as in "I sorta want to go back to school, but I'm not sure." Your explanation takes as long as a minute or two because you aren't exactly sure about all of the specifics. By the time you finally get it out, the person is passed out on the floor because you bored him to death. It took you a long time to state your goal, because it isn't clear to you.

Clearly state your goal in a positive and succinct way. Even if you aren't 100 percent sure you can do it, avoid words like "maybe" or "possibly." If you think losing earning extra income would be good for you and that you might want to make it a goal, say or write:

I want to increase my income from $3,000 a month to $3,600 a month.

Author Brian Tracy, whose books I'll discuss in an exercise for this chapter, also suggests you put it into present terms as if you've already completed it. Here's an example:

I have increased my income from $3,000 a month to $3,600 a month.

Step 2: Set a Deadline

A lack of a deadline can make you put off really trying to complete the goal. I understand that there can be a lot of fear associated with failing, but as light bulb aficionado Thomas Edison could tell you, there's much to be said about failure leading to ultimate success. Add a deadline to your goal to enhance the clarity even further. This can be a particular date, a month, a year, or even a lifetime goal. It will be easier, though, to start with a few goals you expect to attempt in the near future. For example:

I want to increase my monthly income from $3,000 a month to $3,600 a month by June 2012.

I suggest adding a deadline to all of your goals. Even if you aren't able to achieve it by the date, you can change the date later, but there's something about listing the hopeful completion time that will kick your subconscious into high gear.

Step 3: Identify the Obstacles

Here's the good news: this is a step that most of the general public does fantastically. Here's the bad news: identifying the obstacles of their goal setting is what usually stops them from trying to achieve their goals in the first place. By pointing out the things that are in the way of a goal, we can figure out ways to overcome them. This is not the path of least resistance, people, this is where the work comes into play. We have goals because they are worthwhile, not because they're easy. Jim Rohn has a great quote about football for this situation.

"Say you're in an empty football stadium. You have a ball and you tuck it under your arm and cross the goal line. Should you feel good about yourself? Did you just score a touchdown? No, of course not. There was no resistance, no other team, no fans for either side cheering or booing you. All you did was walk with a ball on a field. Now, add in the game and the packed stadium of fans. If you cross the goal line with the ball, you have scored a touchdown and you will be cheered and congratulated by your team and fans. This is because you've actually accomplished something. You achieved a goal despite the obstacles against you. You did something that was worth it."

Don't just go for the easy stuff. Push forward and take on goals with a few obstacles. Let's go back to the income goal. What could be a few obstacles?

I'm not due for a raise until May 2012.

I work 60 hours a week and I'm too tired to do much of anything by the time I get home.

I can't work on the weekends because I'm usually too hung over from my drinking on Friday night.

You don't have to figure out how to beat these yet (that comes later), but even just listing some of these on a piece of paper makes them tangible, real things. Thoughts in your head are a lot tougher to beat than words on a sheet of paper. Listing your obstacles is a great first step to overcoming them.

Step 4: Identify the People, Groups, and Organizations that Can Assist

I know a lot of people who are afraid to ask for help. When you're trying to achieve your goals, this is a bad time to play the part of the shy or independent person. Some of the greatest minds in human history had wonderful mentors and assistants to help them get to where they are. A good number of them also belonged to organizations that honed their skills and aided in their achievement of their important life goals. For an income goal, there are books on the subject by authors like Suze Orman and Dave Ramsey. There are also local finance groups or seminars led by speakers who have achieved a great deal of financial success.

A simple Google search will yield wonders. The important thing here is to search. Whenever I'm embarking on a project that requires information beyond my own, I ask somebody who is an expert on the subject. Finding these people saves me tens of hours of my time trying to figure something out myself. For example, when I looked into earning more income from my writing, I looked toward bloggers that had already accomplished my goals. From them, I found out about using advertising on my blog, self-publishing my writing into eBooks and a ton of other useful information.

Make a list of the people, groups and organizations that can help you in your quest. If you can't identify more than just a couple, do a little bit of research. Your goal is worth the amount of time you put into it.

Step 5: List the Benefits of Achieving the Goal

This is the fun part where we can let the imagination run wild. List as many benefits as you can think of to setting and making this goal happen. If you want to earn an extra $600 a month, think about how much more you will be able to do with the extra cash. Maybe you will be able pay down that credit card or student loan more quickly. Perhaps you will be able to afford that new restaurant in the city, or take your significant other on a nice trip. Whatever your goal is, go to town on writing down all the possible spoils of making this goal a reality.

Step 6: List the Skills You Need to Acquire to Attain the Goal

This is another tough part but it is also worth it. Our ability to take on these goals is directly related to what we can do to make it easier and more achievable on our parts. Before starting on self-publishing my first book, I needed to learn enough about formatting my books for Amazon and how to advertise them to Kindle users. Before I could bring traffic to my blogs, I first had to learn all about keywords, search engine optimization and some basic HTML programming.

Perhaps you need to learn web design or a sales technique to up your monthly income. Or maybe you need to learn how to iron your clothes better to look professional for that upcoming job interview. There are so many books available on so many subjects, and there is a growing "how to" directory of videos and articles on the Internet. Many different skills can be learned. If you need a skill to improve your chances of accomplishing a goal, you have little-to-no excuse. Take the time and learn.

Step 7: Develop a Plan

You know your goals and when you want to achieve them by. You know what's in your way and who can help. You know how much these goals will benefit you and you know what skills you must acquire to help you along the way.

Now comes the little matter of "how."

I suggest a detailed plan of the next week and how you are going to integrate these six other steps into your daily routine. When will you put in the thirty minutes in the library researching the right book for a skill? When can you set up a meeting with that potential mentor about his or her expertise? Is there a good twenty-minute period of downtime for you to visualize some of the benefits you may receive?

Schedule the time for this goal achievement to happen. If you never schedule it, there is a good chance you will never move forward. If you slip up a few times and you don't get some actions completed when you planned them, just change the deadline and try again the following week. The best plans are often adjusted many, many times before the end result is reached. You must create a plan to ensure that you will at least attempt to realize these goals.

There is nothing quite like setting up a goal using this process and then achieving it. When I embarked on publishing my first book, I had a boatload of self-imposed fears and doubts. When I actually went through the process of bringing the goal into reality, I felt strangely powerful. Through most of my life, I had created goals, but most of them were related to school or a job. I hadn't truly created the goal from start to finish. I was working on the goal because of someone else or something else. But with publishing my book, I wanted to do something and I accomplished it. I'd always wanted to be a writer, and because of the goal I'd set up, my vocation came into being.

Here's a fortunate caveat to goal setting. When you complete the goal, you cannot help but feeling happy. If you revel in your goal too long, however, that happiness can quickly sour. When you are close to completing a goal, it's best to start formulating a new one so that you can build off of your productive momentum. Sometimes you will get in a rut after finishing a few of these goals. I fell into a several-month lull a few major goals after my first book. That being said, because of the momentum of completing those goals, I finished three more books and despite the rut, I was able to reap the rewards of my goal accomplishment. Even if you have a motivational hiccup, everything you accomplish beforehand will continue to count toward your success.

The Secret to Doing the Work You Love: Purpose

How many of you can say you have a purpose for your life? You might think to yourself, "people like Ghandi or Mother Theresa may have had a purpose, but that's not the sort of thing for an office jockey like me to even think about." If setting interesting goals for yourself can contribute to your work-related happiness, then finding a purpose is extremely important for you, no matter what line of work you're in. A strong purpose acts like an umbrella that protects your goals from the rain and wind of obstacles. In turn, all of your goals should fit underneath this umbrella. For instance, if your purpose was to "create a world of beautiful designs for future generations to marvel at" you would probably work in something like architecture and the goal of "getting a building approved at my firm" would fit under the umbrella, while the goal of "starting a bluegrass pop rock fusion band" might not.

Having a set of goals is like having a cell phone that you can use to call for directions and to tell other people what you're up to. Having a purpose is like having GPS on that phone so that you're certain you're headed in the right direction. If you don't have a life purpose, you may occasionally feel the sensation that you're drifting and that your life doesn't have nearly as much meaning as it should. If your life purpose is superficial or its been chosen for you by someone else, you may feel like you don't have a lot of control in what you do from day to day. The best way to take control of your work life and to improve your happiness in this area is to come up with a purpose for yourself.

My favorite purpose generation tool comes from blogger Steve Pavlina and his website *Personal Development for Smart People*. In his article "How to Discover Your Life Purpose in About 20 Minutes," he describes a method that I've personally used to come up with a direction for my life. Take out a sheet of paper or open a new word processor document. Write down a one- to several-sentence idea of what you think your purpose could be. The chances are that what you've written might be close but doesn't really inspire you or make you excited. Try to get closer to that inspiration by moving down to the next line and revising your purpose.

Keep doing this until you get to a statement of purpose that makes you feel extremely emotional. The kind of statement that gives you the reaction, "Holy crap, if I actually lived my life this way, I would be blessed and happy every moment of the day." Obviously, it's tough to get to this point from a simple statement, and Pavlina suggests that you write over 100 different purpose statements until you get to the winner.

After writing for what seemed like hours, I came up with my purpose: *"I inspire myself and the world with my achievements, attitude, motivation, physique, energy, actions, words and love every single day."*

I wrote my purpose on a small piece of cardstock, cut it out and placed it in my wallet in front of my driver's license. As a result, I look at it to remind myself nearly every time I open up my wallet.

I can't tell you what your purpose is going to be or what it will resemble. You will know what it is when you come upon it after several dozen missteps. This purposeful statement is what you should gear your life toward. Not the almighty dollar, not the promotion, not the pension, but the purpose. This is a much more effective path to happiness than hoping and wishing that you could stumble upon a better direction for yourself.

Actually Doing It

Now here's the hard part. This is the part where I try to convince you that doing what you love is more important than money. In this section, I'll try to argue that people who tend to follow their purpose and who love what they do tend to enjoy life more and earn more money doing it. I'll try to quote from books like Tom Butler-Bowdon's *50 Success Classics,* which said while discussing people's opinions of millionaires, "'Of course they love their work, they can do what they want,' but few appreciate that it was their love of their vocation that helped to make them wealthy in the first place." I'll attempt to point to famous people like Richard Branson (Virgin Megastore and Airlines), Sam Walton (Wal-Mart) and Jack Welch (former CEO of General Electric) who did what they loved and become wealthy from the pursuit. I may even stoop so low as to bring up Henry Ford (Ford Motor Company), who was asked to give up his dream of manufacturing automobiles for a high-paying job, or Michael Dell (Dell Computers) who was told by his parents to give up this computer nonsense and concentrate on being a doctor. These people all chose to stay on their own paths, and they thrived.

Then again, maybe I'll skip all of that stuff and just hope that discovering your purpose will be enough to push you in the right direction, career-wise.

Workout for Money and Happiness

Exercise #1: Rewrite Your Goals

One of the foremost experts on goal setting in the motivational circuit is speaker and author Brian Tracy, who has written such books as *Maximum Achievement* and the appropriately titled *Goals!*. In the latter book, Tracy outlines a goal-setting practice that I've used myself to great success. If you are trying to practice goal-setting in your life, as you should if you desire workplace happiness, rewriting your goals is one of the best ways to make it habitual.

Start this exercise by purchasing or procuring a small notebook and a pen or pencil. Write down 10 to 15 goals that you would like to achieve soon or in the foreseeable future. Tracy suggests then transferring those 10 to 15 goals onto index cards that you can carry around with you everywhere you go. A friend of mine made this step even more portable by using one small card and writing all her goals in a tiny script and placing it in her wallet. However you do it, make it a habit to review your goals whenever you have a chance, especially before you go to bed.

In the morning when you get up, flip to the next page of the notebook and write your 10 to 15 goals from memory. You may forget one or two of the goals or alter one of the existing ones. This may be a case of sleepiness or it may be that one of the goals just isn't as important as you thought it was. You can be the one to make the judgment call on that. Regardless, repeat this process daily of writing your list of goals in the morning and adjusting your index cards if any goals happen to change. Make sure to review your goals one last time before you go to sleep so that they can swim around in your sub-conscious at night.

Studies have shown that people who have goals, especially written ones, tend to be more successful and earn more money. Making this exercise a part of your career-related happiness workout plan will go a long way toward making you both successful and blissful.

Exercise #2: Enthusiasm

In the book *How I Raised Myself from Failure to Success in Selling*, author and former professional baseball player Frank Bettger described one of his secrets to success. Simply by increasing his enthusiasm while he played ball and later when he sold insurance, he was able to raise his income until he was at the top his respective fields. If you like your job and want to increase your income the old-fashioned way (by being better than everybody else in at least one key aspect), enthusiasm is not only an effective solution but it can help you to experience more happiness at work.

Steve Pavlina wrote about an interesting concept on his blog, *Personal Development for Smart People,* that has stuck with me for a long time. He suggested that if you want to thoroughly improve a certain aspect of your life, you should imagine that a person who was an expert in that field has taken over your body. Then imagine that person used his skills and knowledge to get this new body of his back into shape in that area. The easiest example is ask yourself what a world-class Olympic athlete would do if he were transported into the body of an excessively overweight individual. The athlete would begin to eat correctly and train like a madman until the formerly overweight body was whipped into shape.

For this exercise, I'd like you to imagine that the most enthusiastic person in your field of work has taken over your mind and body. Think about how this person would act in certain situations in your work place. Would this beacon of workplace enthusiasm grumble when receiving a hefty incoming pile of papers? No, he would accomplish it with gusto! Would he bicker with his co-workers during a meeting, stating all the reasons why an idea couldn't be done? No, he would praise the idea and attempt to build on it with additional suggestions!

Even if it feels a little fake at first, let the enthusiastic person take over for a little bit. Studies have shown that even if you pretend to be enthusiastic, you will start to feel genuinely enthusiastic. Try to let the enthusiastic persona take over for fits and spurts throughout the day and write down your observations of how you have felt and how your co-workers have treated you differently. Even a small burst of enthusiasm every day can make a big difference with your emotions and your income.

Exercise #3: The Eulogy

When I first started reading and listening to self-help and success books, I was convinced they would be full of namby-pamby Pollyanna "look inside yourself" kind of exercises that would leave me feeling as if I'd just eaten a whole box of pink granola. Imagine my surprise when the book *7 Habits of Highly Effective People,* by Stephen R. Covey, Ph.D., suggested that I think long and hard about my death. While Covey doesn't relate this exercise directly to the workplace, I think it is particularly fitting to think of for people looking to make a financial impact on the world.

Imagine that some amount of time down the line you have passed away. Your family and your friends are gathered at a beautiful ceremony for you. Your loved ones have all decided to say a few words about you during a series of eulogies. What is it that you want them to say about you? Think in your head or write down some of the highlights from their kind words about your living days. Now, evaluate these words for their validity.

Were you actually a pleasure to work with who tried to help clients like they were family? Did you work hard but make sure to put family first? Do you actually live up to the kind words that you want people to say about you during your eulogy? If so, congratulations on being a very successful person. If not, it is up to you to live up to those words. It is up to you to change the way you act and your direction in life to meet these high standards you're setting up for yourself. Only you can change the way people see you by putting these changes into practice during your lifetime.

While it's a little bit strange to think about death so prevalently, it can be completely empowering to think, "I've really fallen short in this area, but I want to be remembered differently at the end. I want to make it happen." Try eulogizing yourself in a different aspect of your life every week and push yourself to live up to these lofty expectations. This will push yourself into being the person you've always wanted to be. The closer you get to this set of goals, the more at peace with yourself you will become.

Exercise #4: Talking Purpose

To accomplish this exercise, I suggest first using the purpose generation tool I mentioned earlier in the chapter. In this drill, you will talk about your purposeful findings with your most optimistic and empowering friends and loved ones. All of us tend to have at least one person in our lives who seems to be a bit more positive than the rest. Even if it's a co-worker or an acquaintance that you don't know very well, any person who isn't going to shoot down your thoughts as impractical is a good candidate for the exercise.

Set up an informal get-together with this person or a few people that fit this optimistic bill, such as a lunch or a brunch. Early on in the meal, casually bring up the purpose tool (that you read about in this fantastic happiness book) and tell them what your findings were. If you picked an encouraging enough friend or group of friends, you will be able to talk openly about this purpose and how you think you're going to apply it to your life. The most important part of this chat is to get some feedback from a neutral party to help you to understand it better.

Here are a few questions you might ask this person or people to get feedback:

- How do you think I can make my purpose a part of work when they don't exactly fit together?
- What would you do if this were the direction you wanted to go?
- What are some ways you think I could start working on this right now?

Give and take is important with this conversation and you may want to ask the other people in the conversation what they think their purposes might be. This can be very helpful and resembles a "mastermind," which I'll be talking about in more detail in Chapter Six.

It may be odd at first to talk with other people about something that is so personal to you. But nothing else will flesh out hidden aspects of your purpose like a conversation with a separate voice can. I love discussing such deep matters with friends and acquaintances because it enables me to get a completely different perspective about such an important subject. Different minds work differently and an idea that you might not be able to come up with for weeks or years might be on the tip of the tongue for another person. When you chat with other people about your purpose, it will be much easier to form the goals you need to form to start living your purpose every day.

Try scheduling this meeting with different people each time to get as many perspectives as possible. If you want to try this with the same people each week, check out the mastermind exercise later in the book for further guidance.

Exercise #5: Passive Income

In this chapter, I've talked a lot about finding love in the work you're doing and finding work in the areas you love. While the former comes from setting positive goals and working on your enthusiasm, the latter can be difficult if you require a certain level of money in your life. Many people do not go for their dream jobs because those jobs simply don't seem to pay enough. I believe that more people would be willing to transition into a field that they love if they were simply making a little bit (or a lotta bit) more money to tide them over during a difficult career move. In my transition to a full-time writing career, the answer was having multiple streams of income.

From a young age, we are trained to believe that a job is what gives us money. We work for a certain number of hours and we get paid X amount for each hour. If we want to get more money, we think that we have to work more hours, like getting a second or third job and spending more time working. I had a friend back in my coffee shop days who worked nearly 40 hours at the coffee shop a week during the day and then another 40 at a copy/office center during the overnight shift. I wouldn't wish that amount of work on anybody. If only he had known that multiple streams of income can mean one active stream of income and multiple *passive* streams of income.

Passive income is money that you can earn at any time of the day (even while you're sleeping) without actively doing work while you earn it. With passive income, most of the work you do comes up front, such as creating a book or other product that people can buy online or in a store. For example, it took me over 100 hours to put together my first book and at the time, I was unpaid for those hours. With the number of copies I later sold (and continue to sell) through Amazon, Barnes & Noble, Apple and other retailers, my hourly rate ended up being well over $100 per hour.

This exercise is to create or obtain a source of passive income. There are many forms of passive or semi-passive income, such as investments, creating products and earning royalties, making a website, real estate and creating a business for someone else to run. There are some start-up costs with passive income and they require a lot of work at the outset. But if you do the appropriate research and put in the time necessary, you can begin earning a greater income that may increase dramatically, depending on how successful your passive income source becomes.

Here are the steps of a successful passive income endeavor:

1. Research the source of income (i.e. in creating your own book this would entail learning all about self-publishing and marketing).

2. Work on your passive income source (i.e. in real estate this might involve searching for a rental property, finding an affordable, local property manager and discussing the financial ramifications with your bank).
3. Deal with sporadic issues (i.e. in creating a blog, this could be deleting spam comments and responding to e-mails with questions or future income opportunities).
4. Set it and forget it (with an occasional check-in).

Not all passive income endeavors are successful, but if you pick a relatively low-risk one like creating your own product, there is little chance that it will affect you negatively. If your passive income source is successful, however, you may be able to work less hard and earn more money. To help you out, I've created a passive income opportunity with this very book. Check out Appendix 2, near the end of the book, for more information.

The Plan

This is an interesting mix of exercises, because some like Rewrite Your Goals are most effective when they're done every day, whereas you may only need to do an exercise like The Eulogy once for it to have a strong effect on you. Either way, after a few months of this plan, you should feel as though you're leading a purposeful and enthusiastic life with a separate source of income bubbling under the surface and ready to supplement your lifestyle.

Monday: Start the week with Rewrite Your Goals

Tuesday: Rewrite Your Goals followed with work on your Enthusiasm in the afternoon. In the evening, brainstorm on your Passive Income source

Wednesday: Rewrite Your Goals with a midday purpose boost of The Eulogy

Thursday: Same plan as Tuesday with Rewrite Your Goals, Enthusiasm, and Passive Income

Friday: Rewrite Your Goals with a Talking Purpose session scheduled for lunch

Saturday: Rewrite Your Goals and some Passive Income work

Sunday: Rewrite Your Goals and analyze what you came up with for The Eulogy again

Final Thoughts

Goal setting and purpose generation are paramount to having a happy and fulfilled work life. Stephen Covey refers to completing a goal as heading in the right direction while cutting through an overgrown jungle. Meanwhile, having a firm purpose in mind is like climbing up a tree and making sure you're in the right jungle in the first place. Don't keep cutting down the trees in your way until you confirm you are going where you want and need to go in life. In addition, adding passive income to your financial situation can give you the added freedom you need to focus on your new purpose-filled existence. Hmm, having a purpose to push toward, added sources of income that can pay out while you sleep and more freedom to do what you want? Sounds like a delicious recipe for happiness to me!

CHAPTER 3: TRUE LOVE AND CONTENTMENT

As a person who is still dating his college sweetheart, I know the joy that can come with finding true love. Some of those who find that wonderful person before, during or after college are quick to want to start a life with that beautiful soul. This may result in an early-twenties marriage and a desire to speedily start a family. There are those who are strongly against such a practice and there are those who have planned to do this their entire lives. I'm not going to make a judgment call either way.

What I am going to say, however, is that sharing love with another person is far more satisfying if you already love yourself. If you are trying to latch on to this shared love as some sort of replacement for something in your own life, you may find that this other person is not the answer to your problems. For instance, if you are desperately looking for self-confidence and you strike up a relationship with a person who has enough confidence for the both of you, you will still need to find your own confidence if it was what you were looking for in the first place.

Everybody is going to have a different definition of love – that's the beauty of it. My definition, for what it's worth, is a connection between two people who have determined they are willing to grow both together and separately. They acknowledge that each will change over time and they don't look down on each other for it. Each of them wants to ensure a successful life for the other, but not at the sacrifice of either of their purposes.

I don't think that love is always easy and I know that tough times occur every so often. People in love need to know how to "fight right," as *The Happiness Project* author Gretchen Rubin calls it. They need to learn that love isn't about expecting certain things from the other person and they need to actively care for each other even when one or the other is in a bad mood. When two people are in love, they need to look for the half-full glass even when life is giving them a rough go of it. In addition, I believe that when two people decide to (or accidentally) start a family, they should not try to live vicariously through their children. It's a much better practice to work on your dreams with your partner and show your children that anything is possible if you strive for it.

Loving Yourself

What do you think about yourself? Be honest. Do you find yourself interesting, attractive, cool, inspiring, funny and worthy of good things in your life? If the answer is no to any of those adjectives, why? Are you being hard on yourself or you just sort of an average person? Nobody's perfect, but everybody has some amazing qualities that he or she tends to be the most likely to overlook. If you aren't happy with a certain aspect of yourself (or many aspects of yourself) it makes sense that you'd want to find your complementary doubles partner who could be strong in areas where you are weak. But you need to make sure that you recognize your own strengths and positive qualities.

We live in a world with a lot of negativity. While our parents or guardians tend to have been loving, wonderful people, they occasionally make us feel small. Even though we have great friends that we enjoy being with, they can frequently be crass, sarcastic and belittling. I realize that we're in sort of a "self-esteem movement" with many kids being coddled with the avoidance of "tough love" but not all of us have been sheltered from some rough situations when we were younger that left us meek and feeling low about ourselves. It's amazing to find that one person that seems to really understand us and make us feel as strong as we always wanted to be. The only problem is, we already found that person a long time ago: ourselves. It's always great to have a backup, but it is unfair for us to depend on the person we love for all our positive energy. The greatest source of positive energy is found from within.

Later in the chapter, we'll talk about a very direct exercise to praise ourselves, but until then, look for ways to satisfy your needs for positivity from yourself. If you feel down after a particularly tough day, try finding a way to feel better on your own without laying it all on your partner. A solitary walk and a reassuring internal chat with yourself can work wonders without putting as much pressure on your loved one. I'm not saying to never rely on the person you're devoted to, but it's always better to have two options than one. If you can learn to be happy with who and what you are, even at the end of a difficult time, you and your cohort will have a much better life together.

Learning How to Fight

A friend once told me that being in a relationship isn't about learning how to love one another, it's about learning how to fight properly. Of course, he didn't mean learning which mixed martial arts style you want to use to pummel your partner/opponent, he meant that if you can learn how to effectively diffuse conflict without letting it turn into a cloud of emotional fury, you can survive and thrive as a loving pair. I know what you're saying: "But Bryan, my partner just pisses me off more than anybody else in my life and I can't possibly hold in my emotions!"

I used to think the exact same thing. You could have charged me for arson with all of the (figurative) fires I started in our relationship. I loved my girlfriend but for some reason she just made me angrier than anybody else I knew for what seemed like the dumbest things possible. I tried to understand why. Perhaps it was because we had been so intimate and raw with each other that when we were together our deepest emotions, positive and negative were right there on the surface waiting to be released. Maybe it was because I felt like this person who "loved" me should "love" me at every moment of the day no matter what, regardless of how I acted. Possibly it had to do with my belief that I was "such a loving guy" who'd had "such a tough time" finding love that I deserved to be treated with 24/7 respect and care. Despite any ridiculous reason I could come up with, I needed to find out how to live with this person without completely driving her and myself bonkers.

Surprisingly at the time (though it makes complete sense now), I found revolutionary relationship advice in *The 7 Habits of Highly Effective People*. While Covey didn't come up with the advice himself, he expressed it in a simple enough way for someone even as dense as my twenty-something self to understand. It was the idea of the gap between stimulus and response.

Dr. Viktor Frankl was an Austrian neurologist and psychiatrist who also happened to be Jewish. He was working on his magnum opus right around the time that Nazi Germany came to power preceding the start of World War II. He and his family were taken out of their homes and sent to the concentration camps of the Holocaust. His work was taken from him and his wife, his father, his mother and many others he was close with perished in the camps. Of his immediate family, only he and his sister survived the horrible ordeal. One day in the camps, emaciated and debilitated, he wondered to himself what he had left that the Nazis hadn't already taken from him. There, in some of the most awful conditions that could be foisted upon a man and a people, he came up with something remarkable. He determined that no matter what the Nazis did to him, he could choose how he wanted to react to this adversity.

While similar to the positive explanatory style mentioned in the first chapter, this was much more intense. Frankl discovered that there was a space between stimulus and response, between what happens to you and how you choose to react. He published his findings and the concept of logotherapy, essentially psychiatry that concentrates on finding your life purpose, in the book *Man's Search for Meaning*. According to Frankl and Covey, this gap, representing about a millisecond for most people, can be trained to the point that you can actually decide how you want to respond to adversity.

I don't know about you, but hearing about a person learning to react in a non-angry, non-destructive way to the torture in the Nazi concentration camps sure makes me feel different about getting mad at my girlfriend for not putting the dishes away. But it was not easy at first to put into practice, despite reading this amazing example. I had to undo years and years of mental training. It turned out I was already making a "choice" when it came to reacting to stimuli. The problem was, my choice was to "let my emotions take over completely." This is the choice that most people make, whether or not they know it.

I had to change my choice. At first, when my girlfriend said or did something that would usually make me frustrated, I forced myself to pause. I wouldn't let myself say anything or do anything until I'd given myself a second or two to think. Don't get me wrong, this was incredibly difficult at first. The pathways in my brain were worn like a deep groove in a carpet between these situations and a lack of emotional control. Slowly but surely, I was able to insert this pause permanently. I had literally widened the gap between stimulus and response, giving me an opportunity to choose a much better path. I could choose compassion, love, logic, humor and many other more effective responses than anger, fear and shouting.

Now, keep in mind, this gap between stimulus and response doesn't just exist for preventing relationship battles. It can be expanded to deal with any issues that you'd typically respond to with negativity. Personally, my relationship needed the most personal work emotionally, so I thought that others in my boat might benefit from placing this concept in the relationship chapter. Use it as you see fit.

Great Expectations

Why is it that people tend to get angrier at their loving teammate in life than they do at people they barely know? What is it that hops this short gap between stimulus and response and gets everybody involved so riled up? I'm no love psychologist, but I believe a lot of it stems from expecting certain actions and reactions from our partners. If we do something nice for the person we love, we expect to receive an equal or greater amount of love shown in return. We seem to live in this fantasy world in which no matter what is happening in the other person's life, our partner should let go of all problems, emotions and issues to show us deep and unwavering love quickly and thoroughly. Seriously?

Do we really think that our partner lives in a vacuum with us in which the internal or external world never intrudes? Should we really be so bold as to assume that at every given moment in our partner's lives we should be the most important aspect? I understand that at some points, we will be the top priority, but it seems like most people assume they should *always* be number one on the priority pedestal. It's these great expectations (see what I did there?) that end up as disappointments. When both partners believe they should get such treatment at all times, these tiny moments of affection without reciprocation can eat away at the base of a relationship.

As we just learned from Viktor Frankl, we can always choose a different reaction in any given situation. Since reacting with pain and disappointment isn't getting us what we want anyway, what is the best possible way to deal with this scenario? Should we actively give love without expecting anything in return? According to Dr. Covey, the answer seems to be yes, if you're looking for a happy relationship.

In *7 Habits of Highly Effective People*, Covey talks about the concept of "active love." Covey relates a story of how a man came up to him and told him the love had left his relationship with his wife and he wasn't sure what to do about his family. Covey asked the man if he'd tried "loving her." The man, assuming Covey misheard him, reiterated that there was no love left between the two of them. Covey explained himself. He meant that love was a verb, an action, that one partner gives in the form of empathic listening and compassion. He says that love is not a noun, a vague concept shared between two people. It is an act that one person does for the other person without expecting something immediate in return.

Could it really be that simple? If I stopped expecting love to be bounced back like a ping-pong ball and gave it selflessly would it improve the relationship? The answer was a resounding yes. After having worked on increasing my gap between stimulus and response, my girlfriend and I had kept fighting to a minimum, but there was still a sort of raw feeling like when you've unconsciously gnawed on your cheek for too long. Instead of simply pausing when I was stimulated with "fighting words," I chose to respond with "active love." I listened to her more intently without passing judgment. I looked for opportunities to provide her with something extra like a kind note on her desk in the morning or an impromptu breakfast in bed. Typically, I would have wanted to have my efforts rewarded in kind, but I held my mind's tongue and continued to show acts of love.

Before long, my girlfriend began returning my loving acts. It wasn't immediate like a ping-pong match. It was more like the slowly rising stock of a successful company, occasionally sending checks with returns on interest. The checks were small at first but eventually became larger and larger until my life felt abundant with love. Lowering my expectations in getting love in return actually exceeded my original expectations when it was all said and done.

Gratitude

The concept of gratitude is central to many different aspects of self-help, personal development and happiness books. It could really fit into any chapter in this book, since it is truly a universal requirement for all types of happiness. I've decided to include it in this chapter because I feel like couples often have the most to be grateful for but tend to complain the most as well. One partner comes home from work and starts complaining about the day, which turns into the other partner complaining, which turns into any children in the house absorbing this belief that negativity is an inescapable part of growing up. And while negative things do happen, keeping positive about it all through an unshakable state of gratefulness is a wonderful message to instill in our lives and with our children.

Being grateful means openly expressing the things that you appreciate about your life. These things can be small, like a tasty muffin at the coffee shop, or they can be large, like the fact that you have a loving and loyal partner. If it seems like you don't have anything to be grateful about, find things about the world to show gratitude for. Many people are grateful for pleasant weather and then are down and out when the weather is gloomy. It's better to be grateful for all types of weather, thinking that rain will be helpful for the plants and animals in the area and that snow will give people a chance to be inside with their families and for bears to hibernate (and stop eating us). Being grateful is like being a public relations agent for yourself – it's all about finding a way to put a positive spin on your own existence.

If you can insert little bits of gratitude into your day, you are likely to have a healthy resistance to the negative circumstances and people around you. If you and your partner can be grateful about your life together, you will likely be able to handle all negativity challenges the world can throw at you.

Workout for Love and Contentment

Exercise #1: The Mirror Exercise

This is possibly the most New Age-y exercise that I've included in this book, but it is by far one of the most important ones. Earlier in this chapter I talked about "loving yourself," and this exercise is a very direct way to do it. In *Happy for No Reason*, author Marci Shimoff writes about a self-esteem course she took that was taught by the legendary

Jack Canfield of *Chicken Soup for the Soul* fame. During the course, Canfield told Marci about The Mirror Exercise.

Turn on the light in your bathroom and close the door. Take a long look at yourself. Find something that you appreciate about yourself. Perhaps you appreciate your full head of hair near the age of 30 (that's something I'm currently grateful for) or the unique color of your eyes. In a soft, sweet voice, tell yourself that you love those aspects of who you are. Keep searching for external things that you appreciate about yourself, like your clothing or parts of your body. Once you can't think of any more, go into the internal aspects of yourself. Praise your heart, your loyalty and your soul. Always say these phrases in terms of "I love your (blank)" and when you run out of things to praise simply say, "I love you and everything that you are."

As I said, this exercise is very "New Age" and at first you might be worried that someone will walk in the door and label you as crazy. Here's the thing, though. Most people stand in front of the mirror and do the exact opposite of this exercise and are labeled as normal. That's a load of crap. You deserve to think highly of yourself and there is no reason why you shouldn't be able to give yourself as much verbal love as possible. The exercise, while strange at first, can work wonders for your self-esteem and your levels of happiness. It's a great step in the right direction to stop depending on your partner for all of the positive affirmation in your life.

Exercise #2: Solutions Focus

The Solutions Focus is a wonderful problem-solving technique, especially for relationships that was developed by Paul Z. Jackson and Mark McKergow (and written about in the book *The Solutions Focus*) that I first read about in *Happy for No Reason*. For the most part, when two partners are fighting, it's over the aspects of the relationship that are wrong, the ones that are keeping it from being a perfect 10. In the Solutions Focus, instead of concentrating on the parts of the relationship that aren't ideal, you concentrate on what is preventing the relationship from being a 1. It's a wonderful way to show your gratitude for the positive parts of the bond between you and your partner, and it can be used to snap you out of most fighting situations.

Here is how it works:

1. Have one partner ask the other, "On a scale of 1 to 10, how happy are you with the relationship?"
2. If the answer is anywhere above "1," ask that same partner what some of the things are that keep the relationship from being a "1."
3. Now the other partner should share his or her number and talk about reasons why the relationship is above a "1."
4. If either of you answered a "1," what are some tiny things the two of you could do to increase the relationship by a single point, not all the way to 10, but just one point.
5. If you answered above a "1," begin taking some of the actions you discussed in steps two and three. If you answered a "1," take some of the small steps discussed in number four to increase your number.

So much of the happiness in a relationship depends on how each partner focuses on different aspects of the connection. If you two always focus on the negative things that keep you from being a "10," you are bound to be unhappy. Using Jackson and McKergow's brilliant technique, however, you can start to focus on what works between you and what makes you two know that you're in love.

Exercise #3: Proofs of Love

This exercise is adapted from the wonderful book *The Happiness Project,* by Gretchen Rubin. Rubin spends one of her 12 months of happiness specifically on her loving relationships, and one of my favorite parts of the book was when she made more effort to show "proofs of love." Proofs of love are ways in which you express your love to the important people in your life. These proofs can be as small as a cute e-mail with a funny joke (instead of containing a laundry list of things to do), a text message in the middle of the day or a prolonged hug upon returning home from work. Obviously, the proofs can be as large as an expensive new car (I hope my girlfriend is reading this) or a fancy piece of jewelry, but the best things in life are free and there is no need to always prove your love by breaking the bank.

The belief that you have to "prove your love" might ruffle some people's feathers. They might say, "Well, if my partner doesn't know that I'm in love with him/her, he/she obviously isn't paying attention." To you folks, I have to say, "Suck it up and deal with a relationship in the real world." Just because you went on that fabulous vacation and you take out the trash every day doesn't mean that your partner sees that. We tend to show love in different ways, and if you show love in a way that your partner doesn't understand as love, then it's worth going above and beyond to make sure the message is getting through. Also, it's not like there's a finite amount of love to go around. If you love person, you should show it in abundance, not reserve it for special occasions like fine china.

Make a conscious effort to insert additional proofs of love into your daily routine. According to Rubin, 47 percent of people are more likely to feel close to family members and loved ones if that person is more openly affectionate. So at the least, you may be ensuring more proofs of love headed back your way if you show them in the first place. More than worth it, in my opinion.

Exercise #4: Gratitude List

As I mentioned earlier in the chapter, it can be easy for a couple to fall into the pattern of complaining about many different aspects of their lives. One of the most effective ways to counteract this tendency toward negativity is to schedule some time for the two of you to talk about things you're grateful for. Set aside something like 15 to 20 minutes before one of you goes to work and take out a sheet of paper and a pen or pencil. It's really helpful to actually write this list down so that if you ever get stuck coming up with new things, you can always refer back to things you have been grateful for but have forgotten somewhere along the way.

If you can't think of anything right off the bat, here are some suggestions:

- Be grateful for the technological advances you have at your disposal
- Be grateful for your health or your health relative to some people in the world
- Be grateful for the elements of nature that are near where you live
- Be grateful for having friends and family members that care about you
- Be grateful for having a wonderful partner who loves you

Try to think of new things to be grateful for every day so the process doesn't get stale, though it's perfectly fine to repeat some items if your gratefulness for them still holds some emotional weight. It's also not a problem if you get carried away and continue to talk about things you're grateful for past your original 15 to 20 minute window. Even if there are a lot of problems between the two of you and in your lives, creating a list of things to be grateful for can seriously boost your level of happiness. If you think your children might enjoy being a part of the exercise, feel free to let them in on it. Wouldn't it be great if every family had the tradition of expressing copious amounts of gratitude almost every day? Without a doubt, doing so would certainly increase the amount happiness in the world.

Exercise #5: The Highlight Reel

In Tony Robbins' books *Ultimate Power* and *Awaken the Giant Within*, he discusses multiple NLP (neuro-linguistic programming) techniques for altering negative memories until they either become positive or unrecognizable. Personally, I've always thought those methods were a little bit strange, but whether or not they do work, it's important to make sure that we don't let the negative memories and feelings overwhelm the love for our partner and family. The reason that resentment tends to build up between two people (or between parents and their children) is that negative emotions resonate a lot more with the memory. Unless a memory incites extreme excitement and happiness, it will not hold as much weight in your brain as one that provokes fear, anxiety and anger. As a result, many of our mostly happy memories get pushed to the back burner. In this exercise, we will bring them back to the forefront.

The Highlight Reel can be a solo activity or one that you do with your partner and the other members of your family. While a fun activity for all, I see it as a particularly enjoyable one for your children if you have any. Sit down with a pad of paper and either think about or ask your family to brainstorm happy moments from the past week. The first time you brainstorm the subject, it may take a bit of time, but eventually you and your family will become pros at it. Once you've written down at least five of them, then comes the fun part. Choose an artistic way to represent those five memories.

Here are a few ideas that you can use:

- Write a story about the moments leading up to the memory and how everyone felt afterwards
- Create a diorama using a shoebox and toys to represent the people involved
- Draw or paint a picture of the happy memory
- Make a song or a poem that expresses the feelings of the memory
- Record a video of you and your family talking about the memory

You have completely free reign to do whatever you want with these five memories. All that matters is that you are re-expressing the memory in some form. By artistically re-enacting the memory, you are giving it more strength in your brain. In addition, you are putting the thought out there that these happy memories are valued and that you want more of them (see the Law of Attraction in Chapter 6). Do not be surprised if, after a few weeks of trying this exercise, you start to notice happy memories coming more frequently. Studies have shown that people who research happiness tend to be happier. I imagine that would go almost double for researching the happiness in your own life.

The Plan

This collection of loving exercises may allow you to learn to love yourself, your partner and your family with more gusto and will give you a sense of appreciation for what you have. All of these can be instituted as daily practices, but if you tend to get overwhelmed integrating too much into your life at once, try to focus on one exercise until you master it.

Monday: Begin the week with the self-loving The Mirror Exercise

Tuesday: Find some ways to include Proofs of Love into your Tuesday routine

Wednesday: As the week swings into gear, test out The Highlight Reel with your kids or family

Thursday: Try out the Solutions Focus with your partner to tackle any problems that have cropped up this week.

Friday: Friday is a wonderful time for more Proofs of Love

Saturday and Sunday: End the week with the Gratitude List with your partner or family

Final Thoughts

I used to think that there was something wrong with me. I had always been such a loving person and being good to my partner was always extremely important to me. And yet, despite having someone wonderful in my life, I wasn't happy with the situation and I often lashed out in anger. Many loving people end up in the same boat and don't understand why. Trust me when I say that it's simply a matter of falling into some negative habits. And while I know it's really difficult to break a habit, it's much better to break a habit than to break a family (or a prospective family). I hope that if you are one of the millions who are having trouble loving your partner that these exercises can help. It can take time and there may be occasional relapses (been there, done that), but making these habits of self-love and active love part of your life can make a huge difference in your levels of happiness.

CHAPTER 4: EDUCATION AND JOY

I love ridiculously educated people, and a good chunk of my friends have letters after their names and a plethora of high-paying employers after their services. Frequently, the highly educated have a ton of amazing conversation topics to bring to parties; they are never stuck in the doldrums of "how about that weather?" and "did you see the game last night?" conversational fare. Some ridiculously educated people have had a plan all along and know exactly what dissertations they have to write and what degrees they plan to earn. Others seem to by flying by the seat of their pants, going from program to program, master's to doctorate, learning everything they can and trying to avoid the "real world" as long as possible.

It's that latter category I tend to worry about: the people who spend so much money and energy learning about these high-paying professions that they neglect to spend the requisite time learning about themselves. Some of them do so much graduate work and research that they don't know what they are truly passionate about. This chapter will help to make sure that those in the world of "perpetual education" are able to give themselves a complete education of both their fields and most difficult subject of all: the self.

If you spend a long time focusing on the eventual financial benefit of higher education, as many grad students tend to do, you may forget about the importance of learning things that you like or enjoy for their own sake. Even extremely wealthy businessmen like Felix Dennis, the mega-millionaire who founded popular magazines like Maxim, have a passion on the side. In his case, he spends his extra time on poetry, not something that will earn him an extra degree or gain him a consulting position. Reading things that you deep down want to know about can help to stimulate your creativity and make you feel less stressed about all the work that you have to do.

Many people striving to be educated for education's sake may spend a decade looking for the right blend of letters after their name that would guarantee their potential salary. No matter what you learn, however, you have been given certain natural gifts and your own unique circumstances that may already be what you need to become a major success. Sometimes it's just a matter of looking at what you have and who you are. School can teach you a lot of wonderful things. There are formulas and theories, contexts and biographies, but there is one thing that most schools tend to gloss over. And that is teaching you how to think for yourself and to make time for that thinking in your life. As many opportunities as a perpetual learner might have, I would much rather bet on a perpetual thinker who acts on his thoughts. Lastly, while books and professors may be able to teach you some of the secrets of the universe, it's often when you branch out to other people and cultures that you learn the most and find more effective sources of happiness.

The Basic Questions

I want to preface this by saying that I don't think what I'm about to say fits all academics, but I feel that a lot of people retreat into a world of figures, stats, metaphors and dense text to avoid thinking about themselves and the basics of who they are. They know the answer to ridiculous questions that are too intellectual for me to even guess at, while they would pause at questions like "What do you want in life?" or "What makes you happy?" If research and education makes you happy, that's fine and actually kind of awesome. If you are using it to avoid finding out who you really are, it's worth asking yourself a few of the basics.

Here are a few good ones that you could use to learn more about yourself:

- Who am I and what do I do best?
- Who are the people I care about the most in the world?
- Does what I'm studying fulfill me?
- How could I make my life more interesting?
- What do I want to be doing in five to 10 years outside of my career?

Obviously, people other than academics could learn a lot about themselves by occasionally touching on some of these subjects. The real point of these questions is to make sure that in the middle of a potentially decade-long journey of education, you able to know how you've changed and grown throughout the process. Knowing who you've been, who you are and who you want to be in the future makes it much more likely that you're headed in the right direction for the life you want. Just like writing down a goal makes the chances you'll achieve it go up, writing down a philosophy and the focus you want your life to have later on, improves your chances of living with that world view.

Learning on the Side

There are those who truly love learning and want to remain in school forever. There are also those who are afraid that the things they like to do will not be profitable and if they had a choice between being poor and happy or being comfortable but malcontented, they would go with the latter. I realize that security is important and that attaining security by being extremely well-educated is a lot of hard work, so more power to you. It is my belief, though, that you do not have to give up the things you love to do. In other words, if you achieve your degrees so that you can survive in the outside world, the learning you do on subjects and skills you find fulfilling will help you to survive on the inside.

I have an extremely hard-working friend who earned his Ph.D. in applied mathematics from a prestigious university. He went straight from undergrad to a Ph.D. program and then directly to a postdoc program. The man works hard on his academic career, but he has not neglected working on his passion during all of this. He is also an accomplished saxophonist, and it's easy to tell that if both professions earned him the same money and he had to choose, it would be music, hands down. Despite the countless hours he's had to put into his math career, he has never given up working on his music, even releasing an album about a year ago. Now he has actually saved up enough money to take three months off academia to work completely on his passion next year.

Academics are passionate people who put a lot of their heart and soul into their work. It is for this reason that they can get burned out – they aren't keeping their hearts and souls healthy with the things they love. If you are working on that law degree and you feel overwhelmed, find time to fit in that dance class you adore and, despite having less free time, you will feel the pressure lift away. Use some time to work on that children's book you've dreamed of writing and those difficult doctor's hours will feel much more energized. The world isn't so cruel that it would make you choose to give up every aspect of learning that you love. As many movie stars say about projects that make money versus projects they love, "I make one for them and then I make one for me." Take some time to make that project for you in your day-to-day life.

Acres of Awesomeness

I feel a little bit as if this chapter is almost against the concept of the Renaissance man. The person who fits this bill gets several degrees and takes on multiple careers before settling on a true life's purpose. I find it a bit ironic, then, that the story of a man from the early 20th century who split his time as a writer, a lawyer, a minister, an orator and later a university president ended up telling the seminal tale of looking at what you have to offer instead of hoping to find greener pastures elsewhere. Russell Herman Conwell was a Baptist minister in the Philadelphia area who was approached by several young men who wanted to go to college but couldn't afford any of the schools in the area. In order to raise money for a school that later became Temple University, he went on a huge lecture tour, telling a famous and inspiring story called "Acres of Diamonds" over 6,000 times.

When Conwell was on a trip in the Middle East in what is present-day Iraq, a river guide told him a verifiably true story as they floated along the Tigris River. In the story, a man named Al Hafed was living a wonderful life with a productive farm, a beautiful wife and loving children. An elderly priest visited the man and told him about the formation of the world, including the earth, the stones and the precious metals. The priest said that finding just a few diamonds would yield not one farm but many farms. Hafed was no longer content with what he had and he sold the farm to go travelling across Palestine, Europe and Persia to find diamonds. A few years later he was completely broke, clothed only in rags. When a large wave came in from the sea, he happily let himself be swept away.

The man who bought the farm had a different experience entirely. He was watering his animals in the stream on the property and noticed a shiny stone in the water. He picked it up and placed it on his mantle. When a friend was visiting, he correctly identified the stone as a diamond. The man who owned the farm said that couldn't be, because there were many stones just like the diamond glistening in the water. It turned out the farm was one of the richest diamond finds of all time, the mines of Golconda. The mines would end up yielding not just one diamond, but acres of diamonds.

One of the morals of the story is that we should not assume that all the successful life choices are somewhere else. There is a good chance that your own capabilities and circumstances are already a perfect breeding ground for a lifetime of happiness. All you have to do is look at what you've already got going for you and use it! One of the best ways to do this? Thinking for yourself.

Thinking for Yourself

One of my favorite self help speakers is an iconic character from the 1960s named Earl Nightingale. With a booming voice, he was perfect for radio earlier in his life and later made the transition to television talking about ways that an average person could rise to career success. One of his audio programs, called *Lead the Field*, made a major difference for me, focusing on such important principles as attitude, introducing me to the "Acres of Diamonds" story and teaching me the basics of the Law of Attraction (see Chapter Six). The concept he wrote about that had the most impact on me was something I previously believed I understood quite well: the concept of thinking.

I'd done quite well in high school and graduated with relatively high grades in college, so if you had asked me if I was well-experienced at the art of "thinking" I would have laughed at you and said, "Of course!" Using that idea of thinking, most people with masters and doctorates might have used their brains twice as much as I did with my education. This isn't the type of thinking that Nightingale is referring to, though.

How often do we just sit down and think about our lives? When do we find time to think about where we want to be in five years and where we've been for the past five? When is the last time we thought about how efficiently we do the things that we do, searching for ways to improve our productivity and cut out the fat? As far as Nightingale is concerned, the answers are "Not enough," "Most people don't," and "Probably never." Put simply, we like to think about anything other than ourselves. We will contemplate the theories of Plato and Aristotle, we'll go about proving some complicated integral or quadratic equation and we'll even try to figure out the latest twist in our favorite evening soap opera, but we are not likely, when left to our own devices, to think about how we can do better.

Most people are too busy (or say they're too busy) to find the time to think about much of anything at all, let alone who they are and what they want in life. Don't wait until you're 65 to take some time to think. Get out a sheet of paper or a notebook and spend 15 to 20 minutes thinking a few days a week (or every day, if you can). It doesn't matter what you think about as long as it's related to your life and not some assignment. You never know what ideas you'll come up with, but more than likely, you'll find a way to live life a little more effectively, which is a step in the right direction toward happiness.

Finding a Purpose in People

It can be easy to forget that ideas that may fit perfectly with our lives will not always be found in a textbook or a classroom. Many academics also have a difficult time spending a portion of their time with non-academics. It's almost as if some of them believe that they exist in a completely different world with different rules and that mixing with non-academics would be like combining oil and water. But similarly to how some of the best ideas come at times in which we're completely relaxed in the shower or before we go to sleep, other incredible concepts and life directions may be available to us when we allow the other people of the world into our lives.

Muhammand Yunus was a student in an economics program in the 1950s. He had earned a master's degree in 1961 and even worked as a teacher where he earned his undergraduate degree. Here's the stitch in the situation: he was studying and teaching at Chittagong Collegiate School and Dhaka University...in Bangladesh, one of the poorest countries on the planet. During a country-wide famine in 1974, the economics professor couldn't help but see the emaciated people walking through the streets of Dhaka. How could all of the economics theories he had learned that dealt in millions of dollars be valid, when some of his countrymen were going without food?

Yunus visited the nearby town of Jobra and found that most of the shopkeepers that would typically help build a local economy were caught in a cycle of debt that never let them turn an adequate profit. He found that the first woman he spoke to only earned a profit of two US cents a day and couldn't even buy the raw materials to manufacture her bamboo stools without paying exploitive interest rates. He lent money to 44 shopkeepers, only $27 in total, as an experiment. He believed that with the smallest bit of help, the poor might learn to sustain themselves to improve the country's economy and its citizens' livelihoods. He was right, and he used his ideas to found the Grameen bank, which offers microcredit to the poorest people in the world to help them create a life for themselves.

Yunus took a small trip outside of his city and his status and found an idea that changed the world. By applying his research to people who were not academics, he was able to bring happiness to millions. I'm not saying that everybody in academics has an amazing idea hiding below the surface to the degree that Yunus did, but I am saying that if you allow yourself to fraternize with a diverse group of people, you are bound to learn more about the world and you may find an engaging life purpose. In addition to that, studies have shown that by talking about a variety of subjects with people who have different viewpoints, you stimulate your brain to create the mental pathways needed to let your brain "learn new tricks" (like the exercises in Chapter One).

Your Education and Joy Workout

Exercise #1: My Own Philosophy

In the world of academia, a lot of time is spent on understanding the viewpoints of others or applying very specific skills to problems. There isn't always room for presenting your own worldview. This exercise is an effort to solidify not only how you look at the world but also how you *want* to look at the world. Most goals tend to focus on getting something accomplished or working toward something, while this exercise concentrates on changing your perspective.

Take out a sheet of paper and ask yourself the following questions:

- What do I currently think about the state of the world?
- How could I improve my opinion about the world?
- How do I currently think about people in general?
- How could I improve my opinion about people?
- How do I currently feel about my place in the universe?
- How could I improve my feeling about my place in the universe?
- Any similar questions related to your current worldview vs. how you could make it more optimistic.

We have a tendency to think negatively about life, people and our place in the grand scheme of things until we play around a bit. Since optimism and a positive life philosophy can have a major impact on your happiness, it's important to put your current beliefs out in the open. This will give you the opportunity to change them. When answering the "how could I improve" versions of each question, list three things you might be able to do to craft a more optimistic philosophy.

For example, perhaps you would be able to improve your opinion of people by volunteering your time for charity once a month, by visiting a foreign country or by reading an uplifting non-fiction book. From my experience, altering your philosophy is a difficult task, but when you change it from negative to positive, it's like moving a cloud out from in front of the sun. In addition, putting your own philosophy out there instead of talking about the worldviews of others gives you a feeling of significance and consequence while you study most important people in your field.

Exercise #2: Twenty Minutes for Me

Busy academics, employees and freelancers may know this better than I do, but if you don't schedule something in your planner, it's not likely to happen. This goes doubly when it comes to working on your own projects that you aren't required to do. Some days, I truly have to drag myself out of the house to get working on my writing projects because I don't have an advisor or any official deadlines. The only effective way to work on projects you want to do on your own is to build up your habit of making time for yourself.

Start this process by scheduling a block of just 20 minutes for you to work on something that you love. Plan it at least a week in advance and make that time sacred, not allowing yourself to reschedule it or do anything else during the 20 minute block. Come up with something that you want to do that nobody else is requiring you to do. This means no work, no chores and no sleep during that time. You may have to turn off your computer and your phone and shut your door to make sure there are no distractions. The important part of this exercise is that you are doing something you love or working toward a project that you love.

Here are some examples in case you're still feeling fuzzy about ideas:

- Practicing an instrument that you enjoy playing
- Writing a few lines of a screenplay you've wanted to write
- Getting in a 20-minute jog around the block
- Putting in some time on a model airplane
- Working on your blog of unique Cajun recipes

By devoting even this small window of time to your own pursuits, you will start to make progress on your passion. This creates a feeling like no other and one that work for a boss or a university cannot provide. If you are able, increase this 20-minute window over time or employ it multiple times a week. Before you know it, you will start to look forward to this time geared toward yourself and your happiness reserves will increase.

Exercise #3: Self-Disaster Kit

During high school, I volunteered with a student organization called Environmental Education Club, which involved teaching middle school students about nature, while allowing up to 10 excused absences a year along with bottomless hot chocolate (of course, it was all about the teaching). One of my favorite units to teach was survival. The lesson began with a bag full of items including newspapers, matches, a metal pan and about 15 others. It continued with a scenario that the entire group had been in a plane crash and landed in a remote location (I assure you, the lesson was crafted way before the show "Lost" aired its first episode). The group must agree on 10 items to take from the plane that will best support their chances of survival.

Determining your own "acres of diamonds" is a very similar process in its own way. People will usually go out into the world and try to learn everything they can instead of seeing what skills and abilities they've already got. In this exercise, you will create your own self-disaster kit by listing out your skills and circumstances.

Here is the procedure for creating the list:

1. Write down all of the skills you have (e.g. writing, dancing, sewing, etc.)
2. Write down all of the practical traits of your personality (e.g. extremely personable, unwavering honesty, upbeat and energetic, etc.)
3. Write down practical objects in your possession (e.g. computer, website, large apartment, etc.)
4. Write down all of the helpful people in your life (e.g. parents, friends, friendly acquaintances, etc.)

It can be a bit strange to write down everything that you've got going on for you. It can also be enlightening to see that if your grand plan of life takes a detour, you have acres of diamonds in your own backyard. Once you've created this list, you can add to it periodically, but the most important thing to use it for is to look at it when dealing with the challenges you face on a week-by-week basis. More often than not, you can use your skills, personality, objects or people to take on financial, personal and job-related issues that would usually have you spending too much of your own time and energy. Knowing what you have going for you can also prevent feeling emotions of self-pity and negativity when you literally have a list of all the good stuff in your life at hand.

Exercise #4: Thinking Improvement

Thinking is one of the most important tools for happiness. If you aren't thinking about ways to improve your life and the lives of the people around you, there is a good chance you will stay in the same average or below-average mood level for the rest of your time here. As I mentioned before, thinking for yourself is a skill that you need to develop, especially since most people have never thought for themselves for their entire lives. While I recommend that you find your own way to work thinking into your life, here is one way to do it.

A procedure for Thinking Improvement:

1. Get up 20 minutes earlier than you usually do in the morning.
2. Grab a sheet of paper and a pen or pencil.
3. Decide what you would like to think about during your session and make an effort to keep routine items like your to-do list handy. For example, you may think about how you can improve your health, financial status or relationship.
4. Let a few thoughts come naturally and then build on them with new ideas based on what you can come up with. Continue the process until 20 minutes have elapsed.

I realize that it's a simple process, but just because something is simple does not mean it can't be extremely effective. When I hear the classic statement, "I think therefore I am," I usually think of the rebuttal, "If you don't ever think, what the hell are you?" One answer I can probably rule out is "Happy."

Exercise #5: Network Coverage

I know, I know, I'm probably going to come off like your mom or something when I say that this exercise focuses on going out and making some new friends. As Muhammad Yunus proved with his Grameen Bank project, if you are able to see how the rest of the world works, you may find the perfect application for your particular genius. Now, most of us don't have a destitute village a few hours away from our house, but I'm not asking you to necessarily meet up with people who are in need of desperate help. This exercise is simple: meet people in a social group that is different from your own. We feel comfortable in a group of people with similar interests to our own, but we become more successful and learn more when we find out more about a variety of people through direct social contact.

Here are some examples of groups that you might want to become more familiar with:

- People in the service industry such as baristas, waitresses and bartenders
- People in the arts such as actors, dancers, painters and poets
- People that define themselves by athletics such as runners, bikers, hikers, boxers, baseball players and a host of others
- People in the Armed Services such as the Army, Navy and the Marines
- Those in a different social class, different neighborhood, different religion and/or a different political affiliation

The easiest way to connect with a group that is outside of your normal circle of contacts is to volunteer for an organization or go to a meeting or party with people from that group. You may find it difficult at first to connect, but you can learn quite a bit. There are some organizations that put together trips, giving people with different backgrounds an opportunity to interact. A few years ago, I went to Israel with the Taglit Birthright organization. The group allows people of Jewish descent below the age of 27 to visit Israel with nearly all expenses paid. I was able to meet people of a dozen different professions while seeing an entirely unfamiliar culture. I'm not saying I came back a completely different person or anything, but it was shortly after that experience that I moved to a more freelance writing lifestyle. Seeing people at your age doing many different things with their lives can certainly be an inspiration, and it was just the motivation I needed to make some changes in my life.

One of my favorite Earl Nightingale sayings is that "your income is directly proportionate to your service." If you can find a way to apply your education to the service of others, you can improve your earnings, cement your purpose and increase your levels of happiness.

The Plan

This workout for education and joy includes multiple lists that you create once and then refer to every so often along with exercises that might benefit you by doing them daily. As always, feel free to change up this plan to make it fit your schedule more effectively.

Monday: Start the day with Thinking Improvement, brainstorm how to tackle a problem this week with the Self-Disaster kit

Tuesday: Start the day with Twenty Minutes for Me

Wednesday: Start the day with Thinking Improvement, then work on the My Own Philosophy exercise

Thursday: Try Twenty Minutes for Me in the morning

Friday: Use Thinking Improvement to start the day

Saturday and Sunday: Go on an outing with new people based on the Network Coverage exercise in the evening and add to your My Own Philosophy and Self-Disaster Kit lists.

Final Thoughts

Education can be a wonderful thing. Combining it with a very intuitive knowledge of self, frequent brainstorming and time for non-academic pursuits and you will be a force to be reckoned with as far as achieving your goals is concerned. Most of us want to change the world and frequently it is the highly educated that are most able to do this. Take Muhammad Yunus' lead and find a way to make your education benefit both yourself and the world around you.

CHAPTER 5: GRATIFICATION AND PEACE

Happiness is a term that can be interpreted in a lot of different ways. Most people use it to refer to the little things that make them happy. They say that a walk on the beach makes them happy or playing a sport with their friends makes them happy. They might also say that watching television and playing video games make them happy. I don't dispute the belief that a life that includes walking on the beach and playing with friends might make one person as happy as another person who watches television and plays video games. Doing a lot of little things that you enjoy throughout your lifetime can lead to a pleasantly entertained life.

When I talk about happiness, though, I'm typically referring to fulfillment. Happiness is feeling not only good about your life and the energy and activities that you've put into it but also feeling at peace and connected with the world. One of the key differences between the world 30 years ago and the world today is that today you can find a direct source of entertainment, typically in the form of a smart phone application or a television show, from the beginning of your life to the end of your life. It's now easy to be entertained from womb to grave without much interruption, as I like to say. But is that why we're here? To enjoy every moment mildly with a dull electronic hum in our ears?

Personally, I believe that we will not lead as fulfilling a life if we value these digital diversions too far above moments of silence, peace and inner calm. I think a good rule of thumb is that if something is easy to obtain (such as a free smart phone app), it is less likely to be fulfilling than an activity that is more difficult, such as a moment of serenity in the middle of a difficult week. We live in a fast-paced world with business happening at the speed of light, so we seek these games, drinks and lifestyles that enable us to keep buzzing from the beginning to the end of our days and our lives. I thoroughly recommend a break from the buzz. Lastly, I think that being connected to everybody via e-mail, Facebook and texting is often less fulfilling than actually connecting with people by empathic listening, awareness and a love for your fellow man and woman.

Your Moment of Zen

Let's talk for a second about playing around on your phone, your music device or your television in terms of uppers and downers. When you've had a long day of work, full of staring at a screen in some cases or burying your nose in some books, you probably could use something to calm you down. You might have strained eyes or a tired set of lungs, depending on what you've been working on all day. Even though it seems like the best course of action in this situation is a short nap or a quiet moment with family or friends, we have gotten it into our heads that the first thing we need to do is participate in activities that prevent us from thinking. We think that if we do something like play Angry Birds or watch the latest awful reality show, the lack of thought we perceive in our heads is giving us a much-needed rest.

Here's the problem, though. The reason your brain isn't buzzing with thought is because you're buzzed. You're being stimulated by the flashing lights of a phone or television screen. You're drowning out your brain with loud music or a video on the Internet that's full of kittens. You think that you're giving yourself the rest that you need, when in actuality you're continuing to pump stimuli into an overworked brain. We wonder why we're prescribing Attention Deficit Disorder drugs at an increasingly high rate for our children. It's because they're growing up in a culture of overstimulation. Fifty years ago, we watched television a few hours a day but otherwise we worked or relaxed. Ten years ago, we had both television and the Internet to contend with. Now, it's possible to distract and stimulate our brains nearly all of the hours that we're awake.

Earlier I talked about the space between stimulus and response. Nowadays, whenever we receive the stimulus of a few seconds of quiet alone time, our immediate response is to pull out our phone and check something out on the Internet. This doesn't resemble a healthy habit; it's looking more and more like an addiction. Like a worldwide boycott on a moment spent idly.

I once heard a quote that was attributed to actor Clint Eastwood, in which he said, "Don't just do something, stand there." He was talking about the internal process of acting, but I think these are important words to live by. In an effort to remain constantly entertained and stimulated, I think we're missing out on the simple joy of standing around, looking at people and taking in the amazing planet we're fortunate to be a part of. We are missing out on our moments of Zen and it's starting to affect our overall levels of happiness.

Reflection and Meditation

Imagine that you have just gone through a long day of work. No matter what you did, people kept throwing tasks your way to do and think about for your entire shift. All of these activities you had to work on are like pieces of garbage thrown into the trash compactor of your brain. Despite the fact that you may have been tired and felt overworked, you were required to stuff more and more trash into that rusty, old compactor. Upon leaving work, there is no better thing to do than to decompress, literally getting the garbage out of your head piece by piece. The best way to do this is not with additional stimuli like games and toys, which are actually putting more pieces of garbage in your head. The most effective way to take out the trash is with self-reflection and meditation.

Reflecting on a day or series of tasks that you didn't particularly enjoy can be difficult. The issue is that if you don't let these things out of your head, you can quickly become burned out. This is one of the potential problems that can occur in those who are always connected to their e-mail and who never *truly* leave work. It also happens to those who don't decompress and relax properly. There are a few ways that you can reflect on your day that will contribute to your happiness as opposed to trying to beat your brain into submission with overstimulation.

By taking time to write down your thoughts, as I talked about in the Education and Joy chapter, you can free your brain from the clutches of doing the repetitive tasks of the day. You can also express your feelings about certain issues that may have bothered you or you may be able to generate new ideas to solve problems in a more relaxed setting. Another way to reflect on your day is to talk it out with a friend or other loved one. I know that it's a cliché for two people to ask each other, "How was your day at work?" but actually answering the question can do a lot to spill the beans from our bean-filled heads. If the people you hang with in the evening don't ask such a question (which can happen after years of answering the question with a simple "good" or "nothing out of the ordinary") feel free to ask if you can share your story of the day and how it affected you. Lastly, if you'd rather not write your thoughts down or express them to others, you can give yourself 10 to 15 minutes to simply reflect on the day silently on your own.

Reflection is all well and good and its an important part to giving your brain the break it deserves as opposed to the one the electronics companies have convinced you that you require, but one of the best ways to completely decompress after a long day is through the process of meditation. I'll admit that I'm no master when it comes to meditation. I've heard of many different ways to do it and I'm still not always convinced that I'm using the most relaxing methods. There are many different books and audio programs on the subject of meditation and I suggest that you search until you find a method that works for you.

The two methods of meditation that I've used primarily are what I'll call the "silent internal mantra method" and the "scenario method." In the former, you sit or lie down in an extremely quiet place and you use a mantra that you've either been given or you've come up with yourself. On personal recommendation from Marci, I used the book *The Abundance Book* by John Randolph Price, which is made up of 40 straight days of meditation on the subject of abundance. The plan uses 10 different mantras to meditate on dealing with how you are connected with a divine source of income that isn't connected to your job or to a particular person (more on this in Chapter Seven, when we get to the weird stuff). Not only is the process extremely calming, but by concentrating on a particular thought, your brain is practically lifted to a higher plane of creativity. This meditation has helped me to let out some of my bottled up frustrations, leading to increased peace and mental health.

I've used the latter method from time to time for problem-solving or directly increasing my levels of happiness. In this type of meditation, you come up with a scenario such as having a conversation with a version of you from five years in the future and you let it play out in that creative noggin of yours. In that particular situation, I don't try to control what this future self will tell me, but most of the time it involves phrases like, "you're headed in the right direction, just don't give up," or "you'll figure out that part of your life eventually, don't let it bother you."

Studies have shown that meditation can lead to more activity in the centers of the brain that deal with happiness. Meditation has also been found to reduce stress, increase empathy, lower blood pressure, relieve pain and increase your level of attention, the latter of which is a perfect combatant of the ADD-friendly world we've created for ourselves. If you are looking for a mental break, perhaps a game on your phone or a sitcom will be enough for you. If you want to improve your overall health, including your mental health, in the same amount of time, take up meditation.

A Break from the Buzz

As a former employee of a major coffee company, I feel that I am a bit of an expert when it comes to the benefits and the detriments of caffeine consumption. Personally, I've been coffee-free for around four years now and I have a can of soda maybe once every three months. I realize that there are lots of health studies out there about caffeine. I know that caffeine has been found to decrease the chances of getting Parkinson's Disease, gallstones and colon cancer. I don't debate any of that. The problem is that consuming the caffeine daily in the form of energy drinks and coffee is an addiction and it may decrease your chances for long-term happiness.

We've all seen how caffeine affects our body and brain, seemingly bringing us out of our drowsy haze and making us awake and ready for action. Caffeine works by stimulating the same parts of the brain as cocaine and heroin to essentially block the receptors of the sleep hormone adenosine, increasing production of the happiness hormone dopamine and releasing a whole lot of adrenaline. Caffeine keeps sleep at bay, makes us feel good and keeps us running on all cylinders. If we habitually use caffeine, our body gets used to the drug and requires more to function at the same high level. If we stop using caffeine for even a day after having used it excessively, our body goes into withdrawal and we get extremely sleepy and have a major headache.

This is where I get a little bit angry. People who get a headache when they don't drink coffee for a day blame the "not drinking coffee" for the headache. This is just not true. You got yourself addicted to a powerful drug; the headache is just your body trying to detoxify. It's your body saying, "Whoa dude, I don't know what you've been giving me, but maybe you should lay off for a little while." But we tend to worry about short-term issues a lot more than we do long-term ones, and an espresso or two later we're back in drug-addicted business.

When I began my journey for long-term happiness, caffeine was one of the first things that I kicked out of my life. I knew that a chemical substance that played around with my brain's hormones would not be the ticket to a life of serenity. When I was breaking the addiction, I did get headaches and at first I had difficulty staying awake in the morning. About a month into my detoxification, I noticed that my thinking began to feel clearer, as if someone sucked a fog out of my noggin. Shortly thereafter, my problem of waking up in the morning was completely gone. I felt refreshed at the beginning of every day instead of feeling the need to "get my fix." Without my brain's chemical receptors being all clogged up, I felt happier and healthier.

Here's the thing, guys and gals. A lot of you are probably getting all dramatic saying that your lives will be ruined without caffeine and that you need it to survive. That sure as heck sounds like something a drug addict would say, doesn't it? Maybe you'll even say the cliché line, "I can stop anytime I want to." Try going caffeine-free for three months, see how you feel and spend that latte money on something nice for yourself. If you can truly detoxify and see how wonderful the brain feels afterwards, you'll deserve it.

Selfless Thoughts

Human beings are pretty selfish when it comes down to it. It's not completely our fault — after all, we've been hardwired into being primarily concerned with our own safety. If we weren't, humanity probably wouldn't have lasted as long it has. Since there are no longer wooly mammoths running around that we have to avoid, we can now afford to be a little more conscious of the lives of others. No, I'm not about to tell you to run out on your job for a life of charity and selflessness, though I hear a lot of people who do that for at least of year get a lot of satisfaction out of it. I'm not even saying that you should donate money to charity, even though a little bit can certainly go a long way both for your community and for your levels of happiness. What I am saying though, is that you should start devoting more of your thoughts to the well-being and happiness of others.

In *Happy for No Reason*, Marci tells a great story from one of her "Happy 100" about a woman who was leading a difficult life full of pain as the result of an autoimmune disease. She was dreadfully unhappy and decided to speak to a Buddhist lama to see if he could help her improve her life. The teacher heard her sad story and told her to quit feeling sorry for herself and to concentrate on the happiness of others. At first the woman thought the lama didn't understand her immense pain and hardship, but eventually she tried out his suggestion. She started thinking for the happiness, prosperity and well-being of others as she passed them in the street and on the highway, and she even let a very angry person ahead of her in line at the grocery store. These thoughts and acts of kindness began to make the woman feel a lot better. By ceasing to focus on whether or not other people were making her happy and turning it around completely to wanting to make other people happy, she completely healed her life. Her health improved dramatically but almost more importantly, her mind improved with a major boost in her own happiness.

It's completely natural to think about your own well-being without dwelling much on other people, especially people you don't even know. This is one of those cases where teaching yourself to think in a certain way can make a major impact in how you feel about the world and yourself. Sure, it may feel a little silly to hurl a positive thought toward a complete stranger or to stop to pick up a person's phone after she drops it, but if you string enough of these thoughts and actions together, you will not only feel better but you will also feel more connected to the world around you.

Empowered Relationships

If you're like me, you may have had some trouble at first with wishing positive thoughts to complete strangers. After all, there are some people in the world who don't seem to deserve our feelings of health and wealth. What if we accidentally send a blessing in the direction of a thief or an embezzler? Some of us have even had strangers take advantage of us; for instance, I was once held up at gunpoint and could have had my life taken from me by a complete stranger. That all being said, this doesn't have to be an all-or-nothing proposition. You will lead a happier life if you give more trust and love to people than avoiding them like the plague most of the time.

In another tidbit of wisdom from Steve Pavlina's blog, he discusses his ex-wife Erin's view of people and how they connect with one another in the article "Soulful Relationships." This article helped me to fashion a new view of my relationships with people, in turn, making it easier for me to wish them well nearly all of the time. Pavlina discusses first how most people view relationships with people that they don't know. They believe that there is a separation between people and an inherent risk of rejection in relationships. Most assume that it takes courage to approach a stranger due to potential resistance and that trust and bonding take time. Lastly, they think that forming new relationships leads to an increased risk of being attached to destructive or abusive connections. This mindset isn't so bad for keeping safe and secure in your own bubble, but that's not what we're going for. We're taking the next step to happiness and for that, there is a much more empowering relationship belief system.

Here is Erin's belief of relationships in short: "Everyone you meet in your life — even total strangers — is already intimately connected to you. The idea that we are all separate and distinct beings is nothing but an illusion. We are all parts of a larger whole, like individual cells in a body."

In this seemingly strange way of thinking, the separation between people is replaced by a oneness and a connectedness. There is no risk in approaching strangers, because you're simply recognizing a relationship that is already there. You can feel equality with strangers and your already-established friends, and there is a significance in all the people you pass by. Nobody is inconsequential. There should be no worry in establishing new relationships, because as you release old relationships that no longer sync up with you, you'll find new ones that are a better fit.

When you have a certain way of thinking for your entire life that has been branded into you from birth, it can be a bit strange to adopt a new belief system. When I struggled my first few years out of college, I decided that if I came upon a new way of thinking that might work better than my outdated model, I would at least make an effort to adopt it. Taking on this new thought system for empowered relationships literally changed my life. At first, I was worried because I noticed that some people started becoming less close with me. Not surprisingly, they were the most sarcastic, negative and disempowering people I knew. In a short period of time I connected with my acquaintances a lot more effectively and I felt less worried about talking with those I didn't know. People began striking up conversations with me on a regular basis and some of my relationships grew deeper and more connected.

This is one of the reasons that I avoid slinking into my own little world on my MP3 player or smart phone. I might miss a connection with a person that could turn into a friendship or, at the least, a pleasant encounter. After changing this mindset from independence to interdependence, I found that it was much less difficult to wish positive thoughts of well-being for the strangers around me. Heck, there were no longer such things as strangers, only a collection of friends that you constantly hope the best for.

Workout for Gratification and Peace

Exercise #1: Just Stand There

For our first peaceful exercise for the immediate gratification hungry soul, we are going to pull a Clint Eastwood and "just stand there." In this exercise, we will replace at least one instance in which you would normally grab for your phone, your tablet computer or your MP3 player with the simple act of being in the world. Several places in which this exercise would work include standing in an elevator, waiting for a train or bus or sitting in a car. The exercise is really quite simple:

1. Stop yourself from reaching for your device.
2. Look around at the world around you and ask yourself the question, "How do I feel?"
3. Look inside of yourself and ask the question, "How are things with me?"
4. Stand there in the silence, technology-free for at least five minutes.

If you try this exercise once a day during your work week, you will feel more grounded, more connected with your environment and more connected with yourself. Sounds a lot better to me than checking the score of the game or how that television show ended last night. Peace of mind always wins.

Exercise #2: Subconscious Text Messages

This exercise is adapted from a blog post by Erin Pavlina called "Go To Your Room." In the world of instant gratification, we feel the need to quickly respond to text messages, e-mails, tweets and a host of other forms of communication. One form of contact that we tend not to make is contact with ourselves. In this training session, we will be collecting messages from our subconscious.

Sit or lie down and shut out the worries and problems of the day. I know, easier said than done, but do your best by closing your eyes and focusing on even breathing. After a minute or two of calming down by breathing deeply and rhythmically, picture yourself walking toward an elevator. Slowly walk toward the elevator and press the button on the wall to open it. As you enter, notice a panel of buttons that shows you on the twenty-first floor. Press the button to go to the first floor and begin to feel yourself going down, floor by floor. When you reach the first floor and step out of the elevator you notice a staircase. Walk down the staircase, which has exactly 21 steps. At the bottom of the stairs, you notice a slightly open door and walk through it. You see someone standing there and you ask to be led toward "your room."

You walk into the room and the door shuts behind you. In the room you see a giant chalkboard. It is in this room that you can hold a conversation with your subconscious mind. Ask questions about your life, where you're going, what you're doing and how best to accomplish your next steps. As you ask the question, your subconscious mind will almost immediately begin to write out an answer for you. After you've listened to or read the answers, go back up the 21 steps and to the 21st floor and slowly, calmly bring yourself out of the meditation.

These are the texts that you should really be interested in getting. Since your subconscious mind has the ability to process all of the stimuli you take in throughout your life, it is often a helpful gauge for what the next step in your life should be for any of your unanswered questions. It's a lot more effective at making you feel connected with yourself and at peace than an e-mail link to a kitten video, I'll tell you that much.

Exercise #3: 7 Loving Thoughts

This exercise is based on the story Marci told about the woman, the lama and the selfless thoughts. It can be difficult at first to try to send thoughts of well-wishes to everybody you pass for the entire day. While I hope that you can work your way up to everybody you meet well, let's start just with seven people.

Here's how the exercise works:

1. As you pass someone, send a positive thought, such as hoping that he has a pleasant day and that good things happen to him.
2. When you pass a second person, try sending a different happy thought, such as a series of financial windfalls that leave her and her family well taken care of.
3. Continue to alter your positive thoughts until you reach seven people in total. Others examples of positive thoughts include wishing for the health of that person and his family, hoping that she finds great fulfillment in her day and life, that the

person gains an unwavering optimism, that she wins a fantastic prize in a contest or that he finds inner peace.

Here's the funny thing about this exercise. Even though I cap the number at seven here, you may feel inclined to keep doing it throughout the day because it can increase your overall happiness and your connection with people that you don't even know.

Exercise #4: A Night in the Past

Imagine that you lived in the world over 100 years ago. In this world, when you returned home from work at around 6 p.m., there was no television to watch, no sports scores to check and no e-mails to keep up on. You simply ate dinner and hung out with your family. For this exercise, you will simulate, as best you can, an evening without the typical luxuries you use to "relax" most evenings.

Here is a checklist to make this exercise effective:

1. Prepare your family by telling them in advance that a particular night will be computer-, phone- and Internet-free. Springing it on them all of a sudden might cause a ruckus. Let anybody who might need to get in touch with you know that you will be unreachable as well.

2. Upon returning home from work, unplug the television, phone and Internet, and collect all cell phones in the house and turn them off.

3. With your family, your spouse, roommate or simply yourself, plan out some relaxing activities for the evening. Perhaps you can plan a board game night, some light reading or a hearty conversation.

4. Go to sleep at 10 p.m. or earlier. According to Marci's research into Ayurvedic teachings, "An hour of sleep before midnight is worth two hours of sleep after midnight." The earlier you hit the sack, the better.

This exercise is difficult to coordinate, especially if you have a few rug rats running around. If you can actually accomplish it, however, there are many different benefits. You will gain an appreciation for all of the technological benefits that you have in your life when you shut them off for an entire evening. Secondly, your brain will feel much more alive when it isn't surrounded by mechanical stimuli and especially when you're engaged in conversation instead of mindless screen watching. Lastly, getting an extra couple of hours of sleep preceded by a lack of computerized presence will leave you feeling clear-headed and ready to take on the following day.

Perhaps this will be a mental place you enjoy visiting, even if you don't want to live there. I have a feeling, though, that if you can make it happen once, you will look forward to your "night in the past" as a weekly or monthly fixture in your schedule.

Exercise #5: The Informed Statement

When I tried to institute the new concept of interdependence into my relationships, I wasn't sure exactly how to begin. The way that I started began in my days as a coffee barista, which has had major implications on my social interactions ever since. It began with "the informed statement."

Many people in the world are programmed for a specific type of response in a given situation. Most of the interactions between strangers and people who know each other alike start with a greeting, followed by the question, "How are you?" Because this exchange has become rote, I've seen many people not even respond. This is because it's obvious that you aren't making an effort to connect with this person. Even if you change the tone of your greeting and your question, you'll still probably get the same response.

The informed statement is essentially stating an observation based on a quick survey of the person you are about to talk to and the environment you're interacting in. The "informed" part of statement comes from the emotional and physical cues you can pick up from this "friend you haven't met yet" and other stimuli you can glean from what is going on nearby.

Let me give you an example. In the 2008 presidential election, I mistakenly thought that "voting early" would allow me to quickly get in and get out. An hour and a half wait later in my local library and I had finally gotten to a room that was packed to the brim with people, electronic voting machines and exhausted volunteers. When I approached the table with the ballots, I looked at the volunteer who was about to help me and it was obvious she was frustrated and tired. Wanting to perk her up, I struck up a quick conversation with the informed statement, "I hope they give you guys a break soon."

She looked up at me with a big smile. She immediately started telling me about the dinner they were having delivered and she seemed pleased as punch to have a thirty-second mental break from the tedium. Having been in the final room for the last five minutes or so, I knew that this was the first extended conversation any of the volunteers had engaged in with the prospective voters. When my ballot was retrieved from the folder, she started to read me the required statement, still with a smile on her face. She said, "Now, honey – I mean, voter," and we both laughed. There we were, two friends who'd never met before, connecting because I'd made the effort to see that she was tired and to notice how packed the library was.

Try making an informed statement with people you might not normally converse with. Try it out with grocery clerks, taxi cab drivers, baristas, co-workers, waitresses, parking attendants and anyone else you can think of in an effort to make a more genuine connection with someone. Work on this exercise long enough and you'll begin to feel much more connected with other people and the world around you.

The Plan

The beauty of this plan is that several of the exercises can be easily inserted into spare moments that you have every so often during your day.

Monday: Start your week off with 7 Loving Thoughts in the morning

Tuesday: Set aside at least half an hour in the evening to do the Subconscious Text Messages exercise

Wednesday: In the morning, test out The Informed Statement and try Just Stand There in the afternoon

Thursday: Test out 7 Loving Thoughts in the morning again

Friday: Try A Night in the Past every week or every other week for at least a month

Saturday and Sunday: Test out The Informed Statement and 7 Loving Thoughts each morning, followed by Subconscious Text Messages one or both afternoons.

Final Thoughts

It's so easy to disconnect from the world and from yourself, and in contrast, disconnecting from electronics and other speedy forms of modern entertainment can be very difficult. Separating yourself from your addictions is a very important step in the path to happiness. Adding some of these concepts of self-mastery and friendship to your life even for a few minutes a day can make a major difference in how happy you feel during your down time.

CHAPTER 6: CREATIVITY AND LIFELONG DREAMS

It is truly a wonderful time in the world for the dreamers. Hundreds of years ago it would have been nearly impossible for a creative person to rise up the ranks and become an actor, an artist, a musician or a celebrity for celebrity's sake. Since that time, many restrictions have been lifted from the bottom and the top of the pyramid and a person who has a dream can truly make something of him- or herself. There are even wonderful training schools for all of these professions, giving dreamers even at the elementary school age an opportunity to learn about the arts. But there are also roadblocks.

With more people than ever in the world, some artists perceive that there are fewer spots than ever to go around. In addition to this, whether it be a result of advertising or an increasing amount of negativity in the world, it feels like more creative types are doubting themselves than ever. Being born with a larger-than-normal amount of creativity can already be a burden on mental normalcy, but adding a large dose of pessimism can lead to drug and alcohol abuse, an overactive social life and a belief that working at a coffee shop or restaurant is the closest thing to a creative success you can be.

This subject is near and dear to me, as a writer. In college, I studied to be both a writer and an actor and for a while I also seriously considered becoming a professor-type academic. The creative pull was too much for me, however, and I moved to Chicago with lights in my eyes to follow in the footsteps of comedians like Tina Fey and Bill Murray and writers like David Mamet and Studs Turkel. After a few years of learning comedy from some amazing teachers and writing on my own, I nearly gave up on my dreams because I assumed they would have become reality by then. I'm fortunate to have stumbled upon the fields of happiness and self-help shortly after that time or I might not even be writing this very book. It has been one of my major goals to help those who found themselves high on creativity but low on self-belief ever since.

A creative life is one that must be packed to the brim with hard work. It's almost as if the less difficult classes of college that included movement, set building, drawing, design and acting, when compared to things like particle physics and calculus, are replaced with a need for much more discipline after school than most. Honing your writing, acting or other creative pursuits takes a great deal of time. When discussing the work of Orison Swett Marden, *50 Success Classics* author Tom Butler-Bowdon has a great quote on this subject. "The great violinist Gherardini was asked how long it took him to learn to play. His answer: 12 hours a day for 20 years."

But unfortunately, creative people aren't always exempt from work they don't want to do in order to pay the bills. Some will take service jobs like waitressing, while others will push their sanity to the brink with a 9 to 5 office job. Forty-plus hours a week are tiring for anybody, but imagine trying to fit in "12 hours a day" worth of creative refinement and mastery. I won't say this is easy – it's obviously not – but by learning to manage your energy as well as you possibly can, this attempt to become creatively unique may be more successful, leading to increased happiness.

Many creative folks say that they have a dream, but they aren't always very clear about what exactly that dream entails. They may say they want to be famous or they want to win an Academy Award or some such, while leaving many of the other details about their lives blank. One of the keys to happiness, especially for those with such lofty aspirations, is to be more specific about dreams. If you can plot out many different aspects of what you want in life using processes like creative visualization, you may be able to will your aspirations toward you through the Law of Attraction.

Since it's always best to attack a problem from several different angles, creative visualization is best supplemented by talking about what you want out loud and representing it visually with a vision board. This three-pronged attack can replace instances of thinking, talking and seeing the concept of "not having what you want" with "getting what you want" when you put some positive effort behind it.

Money is always a tough pill for creative types. In the distant past, creative artists were supported by wealthy benefactors so they could concentrate on their purposes. Nowadays, some are sustained by understanding parents or spouses, while others must work constantly in areas they find boring and unfulfilling. Some of the most enjoyable and empowering visualization exercises come from focusing on the money that you want to come into your life.

The human mind is an amazing machine that can come up with most of the solutions you need for your problems and creative quandaries in life. How do you solve the really tough ones that you've been beating your head into the wall about? The most effective method is using a mastermind, which is like a group therapy session for ideas. If you truly feel stuck at a point in your creative development, getting a collection of intelligent, inspired artists together can put you back in the driver's seat for your life.

Energy Management

When I first started reading about self-help and personal development, one of the big buzz phrases was "time management." Though the concept of working more efficiently throughout the day to provide yourself with additional time is a brilliant one, it's pretty difficult to put into practice. While it's obvious that we can be more effective with certain tasks like chores, meals and travel time and that we can cut out certain leisure activities to create additional time in our day, sometimes we'd just rather take it slow to counteract the brisk pace of our 9-to-5 lifestyles. In addition, trying to milk time out of an already busy schedule feels like a one-way ticket to being overworked and tired every single day.

When I came upon the concept of energy management, however, I was intrigued. I already knew that energy was not a linear concept. After all, sometimes I had more energy to work on projects at 5 a.m. than I did just a few hours later, and if I had a clear goal in mind, I was much more efficient than when working on a banal project like an endless data entry assignment. In addition, I knew that my freelance writing days were affected negatively if I'd had a fight with my girlfriend earlier in the day, so emotion had to be a factor.

According to Jim Loehr and Tony Schwartz, authors of *The Power of Full Engagement*, there are actually four different types of energy. If you can make sure to keep your stocks of energy as full as possible, you are more likely to work on your creative pursuits. The four energy types are physical, emotional, mental and spiritual energy. Physical energy involves keeping your body healthy with such actions as eating smaller meals throughout the day instead of three larger ones, drinking enough water to keep you hydrated, getting enough sleep and taking breaks when you need them. You know, all of the stuff we're *supposed* to do but that we tend to sacrifice for speedy and unhealthy choices. Emotional energy deals with a lot of the ideas I mentioned in the previous chapters, such as keeping optimistic, increasing the distance between stimulus and response, believing in yourself and interacting positively with others. Mental energy involves using your brain effectively by keeping it stimulated with creativity, visualization, physical exercise and by building up your mental muscles to handle more difficult tasks. Spiritual energy is partially based on creating a purpose for yourself like I mentioned in Chapter Two, but it's also a matter of showing your true character to the world.

Imagine if you actually put all of these aspects of energy to work for yourself. Think about how much more smoothly your day at work would go if you had the proper food, water and sleep combined with a positive attitude internally and externally – if you kept your brain happy the entire day with creativity and strong mental muscles with a purpose and character driving you to success. Without this energy on an average day, you might get home and want to plop down on the couch. On an energetic day like this, you are going to be ten times more prepared to practice your instrument, go to an acting class, study some artwork, or take on whatever creative aspect of your life you're drawn to. In fact, taking on this creative work can actually stimulate your mental energy for your following work day, keeping the productivity cycle running on high.

There is a fixed number of hours in each day and a good chunk of those are required for sleep. But there is an unlimited amount of energy possible if you keep the machine well-oiled in these four key areas. Getting a chance to work on your dream after you toil on your work is a wonderful way to increase your happiness throughout your day.

Night Owls and Early Birds

To piggyback on the idea of managing your energy, it's important to keep your priorities in mind. Creative people are absolutely amazing and I always have more fun when I'm out with them in comparison to my married or professional friends (sorry guys and gals). Artistic people are friendlier and are frequently greeting you with big, honest hugs. They laugh louder, joke more often and are quick to drink and "party hearty". It's this last area that worries me about creative folks.

The most creative people I know are usually the biggest partiers. They are the least likely I know to have a set routine, and if a night takes them to wild and unusual places, they are apt to go there rather than turn in for the night. Look, I love an adventure as much as the next person and for many, it's these adventures that provide a lot of temporary happiness in the lives of artistic people. I want you to reach further. I want you to be able to feel total fulfillment as opposed to frequent drunken nights of debauchery. I realize that on television you see many movie, music and television stars out on the town getting their rocks off with frequent partying. Those are, of course, the ones you see. The typically successful artists are the ones getting up early and putting in the hours working on their craft.

"12 hours a day for 20 years."

An artistic person should never settle. Personally, I feel strongly that a very talented individual who wastes multiple days in a month (or week) to a hangover just for some supposed networking is settling for a life below his or her capabilities. Talent and passion should be enough in this world, but it's the people who work the hardest who tend to come out on top at the end.

I realize that I probably sound like your mom again, but like a mom, I only want the best for my fellow creative types. I'm not suggesting that you should never go out and have a good time. Friendship and social outings are very important when it comes to happiness. If you make these outings a focus of your life, however, you are going to fall behind the people of your generation who have figured out that hard work and huge goals lead to success. The longer you wait, the farther that you will fall behind. It's time to ditch being the late-night owl and to start being that worm-catching early bird.

Keep Your Dreams Big

Perhaps this has happened to you. You see a giant plate of food in front of you and you decide that you want to eat it all, no matter how your stomach feels. You stuff yourself silly and feel horrible afterward. Then you hear the line from your parents or loved ones, "Looks like your eyes were bigger than your stomach." A few years out of college and I thought that this same concept applied to the goals that I set. It was obvious after a few years that I wasn't going to be an author, an actor or a producer, so I set my sights lower: on getting enough income to survive. While I was looking for the "secure job," I started to feel these pangs of guilt. They were almost like little voices telling me that I still had a chance to live up to my potential. Maybe you've felt them too if you've decided to settle for something below your mettle.

Remember how I said earlier in the book that if I found a belief system that sounded better than my own that I would give it a try? Well, after watching the movie *The Secret*, produced by Rhonda Byrne, I thought I'd try out the Law of Attraction for a while.

For those of you who aren't in the know about *The Secret* or the Law of Attraction, the law more or less states that if you think about something you want to have with a positive attitude, it will eventually come into your life. I've heard it expressed a number of ways, but one of the best ways I've heard it put came from success author Napoleon Hill, who said, "We become what we think about." I know what some of you are thinking the Law of Attraction seems like some cooked up, metaphysical theory that is beyond proof and that only makes money for the people writing about it.

Look, I understand cynicism and being a skeptic. I used to be in that same boat and it was a relatively unhappy one (also, it was sinking. Have I used this boat metaphor too much?). This is a book about learning to be happy and finding a way to achieve your dreams. If I had a choice between being with a bunch of people who told me that I wasn't going to amount to much in life or being with the dreamers, I'll choose the dreamers. I've used the Law of Attraction and it has helped me thoroughly in life. Personally, I think it makes sense in a way. When you put a cell phone next to a computer speaker, you hear a buzz, because the two devices are emitting signals that interfere with each other. When you have a thought, it sends out a signal too that, in a miniscule way, interferes with the universe. If the thought is amplified by certainness and positivity, it is more likely to reach the world at large. Like water washing over a rock formation, the thought soon alters the universe until it comes into reality.

Even if you don't believe in the more metaphysical aspects of the theory, there's another great part to it: your own subconscious. While the universe is changing to fit your thoughts, you are meeting it half way by putting the idea deep into your brain and coming up with ways to make it work. What do I mean by this?

Say one of your goals in life is to become a well-known actress. You put the thought out into the world using the Law of Attraction by thinking of yourself watching a premiere of your own movie, walking the red carpet in a fantastic dress and working on set with your favorite actors. You imagine this life for yourself at least once a day during quiet moments on the bus to work. A few days later, the thought pops into your brain to submit your headshot and resume to that new casting agency in town. You do it and a few weeks later you end getting a call for an audition. The people at the casting agency love you and you end up getting a small part in a scene with a major actor. A thought pops into your head to bring your headshot to the shoot, even though it might not lead to anything. Over a cup of coffee between takes, the actor says he's working on a project that you might be a fit for and you give him your materials...

I realize this is a made up scenario, but I wanted to point out that the Law of Attraction and your own subconscious can work together. The people at the casting agency and the major star enjoyed your work and putting them into your life may have been the work of the Law of Attraction, but submitting the headshot to the agency and bringing your materials to the shoot were demonstrations of your subconscious at work. This is what I mean by meeting the law halfway. Visualize the life that you want and when you have an instinct to take action, by all means, act on it. I fully believe that the Law of Attraction has been a factor of my success as an author and until I'm proven wrong, I'm going to keep using it to create further success.

Words and Pictures

It's rare that you get to speak with a master about your particular art form. You can take classes at schools related to your craft, but it's infrequent that you actually study with someone who has reached the top of his or her field. Usually, the people you work with have achieved some success or have learned about it in a doctorate program, but they've never been "the best." You may take a short workshop with a true master here and there, but during that time you don't usually get a clear answer as to how they went from where you are to where they ended up.

In the world of achieving dreams, however, there have been many books and audio programs released discussing exactly how certain dream achievers made themselves successful. If you apply certain aspects of their formula to your own life, you will get some results out of it. In many of the books I've read that relate to the Law of Attraction or financial abundance, a key practice that sticks out is the use of a vision board.

A vision board is a strange combination between a spiritual wishlist and a middle school art project (which my mom, I mean, I was great at creating). A vision board is essentially a poster that contains pictures of the things that you want to happen in your life. For example, on my vision board I have a graphic that represents my web traffic going up astronomically on my website, another that represents being financially well-off and a large beach-front mansion, along with other images representing close friendships, love, awards, physical fitness and more. Putting together such a collage seems like a silly decoration that you might use in a high school or college bedroom. Of course, just putting it on the wall is not the only thing you do with it.

We live in a world in which we are constantly reminded of what we have and what we don't have. We look at our bank statement with its current balance, we see the decorative state of our apartment or house and we view the condition of our creative career all in real time. One of the reasons the Law of Attraction works is that you put images in your head of what you want to happen. You want to bombard your mind with your future ideal situation because your subsequent thoughts will go out into the world and will shift the universe to move in that direction. If you keep thinking and looking at the things you already have, your brain will continue to send out signals for the universe to stay exactly the same. Boring!

The vision board is one of the most important tools in your Law of Attraction belt. After creating your collage of what you want in every area of your life, you must set aside some time every day to look at it and really concentrate on the images present there with a positive attitude of expectancy. I've heard some pretty wacky stories of vision boards working their magic, several of them in the movie phenomenon *The Secret*. To become a creative success and increase your chances for career happiness, a vision board should certainly be a part of your repertoire.

Creative Therapy

Here comes one of my favorite bits of wisdom that I originally gleaned from the personal development classic *Think and Grow Rich*, by Napoleon Hill. I have personally used this method to build my income, increase my levels of happiness and help other people in my situation to do the same. This method is known as The Mastermind. In a mastermind group, you get together with several people who all want to take their creative projects and lives to the next level. This can be a group of friends, acquaintances, co-workers or anyone at all, and they can be from all different backgrounds. Set aside an hour or two each week for all of you to meet in a location that is not distracting (a movie theater or concert hall would not be a good choice) and have each of you bring your career goals to the meeting.

Start the meeting by having each of the people there go through their basic creative goals and talk about some of the obstacles they've been facing. Have one person at the meeting keep time and set a certain amount of time for each person to talk, so that the entire time doesn't become dominated by a particular person. Either at the end of each person's talk or at the end of the entire group's, leave the floor open to suggestions from everyone present. Those involved in the mastermind can write down the ideas about their lives or they can write down notes about what everybody has said as a whole. At the end of the meeting, the group agrees on a few steps each person can take between now and the next meeting.

Since people don't normally talk about deep, purpose-related subjects, you will be surprised by how many helpful tidbits of wisdom the other folks in your group will have for your life. Other people tend to work more effectively on problems in your life than you can on your own. The mastermind takes advantage of this phenomenon and can help you to make major life progress. It's easy to get stuck when you have such lofty goals because it can be frustrating if a few things don't work out your way. Your mastermind buddies will kick your butt into high gear because they may be able to see the obstacles to your goals from a different angle. With their help, each week you can begin to make major progress with your goals, dramatically decreasing your feelings of frustration and powerlessness.

Workout for Creativity and Lifelong Dreams

Exercise #1: Physical Energy Journal

Many years ago as a health class assignment, I recall taking a 24-hour journal of my eating habits. Of course, I would later do this to the extreme with diets like Weight Watchers and P90X, actively changing those habits as I went. When you think about it, though, it's strange that we don't keep track of other things that affect our physical energy as well. If we are trying to become healthier, which is the goal of most diets, then we should not just track what we eat but when we eat it, how much sleep we're getting and where we're inserting the tiring activities of the day.

For a day or two, try keeping a journal of everything that affects your physical energy. Here are some events that would be worthy of noting:

- Staying up past midnight at a bar or club
- Doing chores around the house
- Drinking more than one alcoholic beverage in a day

- Drinking more than one caffeinated beverage in a day
- Exercising more than 20 minutes in a day
- Doing drugs, having sex, dancing, etc.

Obviously, some of these activities can drain your energy (staying up past midnight), others add to your energy followed by a drop (caffeinated beverages), while others can boost your energy over the long term (exercising more than 20 minutes). If you find that you have been unable to accomplish some of the creative activities you have wanted to as a result of being too tired or experiencing a lack of time, keeping a physical energy journal may help you to determine things you could change that would make your creative pursuit more possible.

For example, when I worked at a coffee shop for the morning shift, I would wake up at 4 a.m. after having gone to bed around 11 p.m. When I arrived at the shop, I would drink a double espresso over ice and by the time my shift was over I was extremely sleepy. I exercised a few times a week, which kept me in relatively good shape, and I rarely drank, but my lack of sleep and too much caffeine made it very difficult for me to concentrate on writing and acting the rest of the day. Eventually, I cut out the caffeine, which made me much more effective in the afternoon. Later, I stopped working the morning shift to allow myself additional sleep. Before I knew it, I was able to write more often and audition for more acting projects.

Try keeping the journal for a day or an entire week to find areas in your life that you can improve upon to increase your physical energy.

Exercise #2: Sleeping Beauty

This connects in part with the previous exercise, but adding to your amount of sleep is so important to achieving your creative goals that it was worth a separate exercise. When you get enough sleep, you are able to be more creative and effective, and in my opinion, there are very few late night activities that are worth limiting yourself creatively for. In addition, there are also factors that make your sleep more efficient, such as giving your brain some time to wind down at the end of the day.

Here is the procedure for the Sleeping Beauty exercise:

1. Pick a day in advance and let your partner, friends and co-workers know that they won't be able to reach you after 7:30 p.m.
2. At 7:30 p.m. on the evening you choose, turn off all the electronics in your house that could distract you from sleeping, such as a cell phone, television or iPod. Literally unplug anything that might tempt you away from this cool down period.
3. From 7:30 p.m. to 8:30 p.m., take part in a relaxing activity. Some examples include reading a book, going on a walk around the block or reflecting on your day.
4. At 8:30 p.m., prepare for bed using your normal routine, minus any electronic interference.
5. Go to bed at 9:00 p.m.

Half of you are laughing right now, I can tell. Some of the other half of you will be so used to getting to bed during the bewitching hour that you may have trouble falling asleep right away. I realize that going to bed really early can cause issue with your social life. Personally, I would rather be successful than cool, and I would rather be happy than cool. I don't always go to bed at 9:00 p.m., and I don't think you have to every night. Since I've started to go to bed earlier, however, I've noticed increased productivity, fulfillment and joy. Try this exercise out once a week (or multiple times in one week) and you will notice a major difference after a few tries.

Exercise #3: Audacious Visualization

One of the things I like the most about the Law of Attraction is that because it's an internal process, there is nobody who can give you a hard time for dreaming big. Similar to Viktor Frankl's experience in the concentration camps, it is your choice how you want to react to what the world has given you. Most people would be resigned to leading a mediocre life after a few years of their dreams not coming to fruition. They have chosen to stop dreaming big because it's too painful or guilt-ridden for them. If you keep dreaming and you associate the dreams with happiness, however, mediocre may turn into extraordinary much sooner than you think.

Here's how the process of Audacious Visualization works:

1. Set aside at least 20 minutes in which you won't be bothered.
2. Sit in a comfortable place, but not one so comfortable that you'll immediately fall asleep as soon as you close your eyes.
3. Close your eyes and think of something extremely positive about your life right now. Try to feel grateful and happy about this circumstance and concentrate on boosting those good feelings.
4. Imagine a circumstance you want in your life. This is your opportunity to think big. For example, as opposed to a small raise at work, imagine your salary doubling or tripling. Carry the feelings of gratitude and happiness over from your previous thoughts as if the circumstance you want is already a part of your life and you're grateful for it.
5. Repeat step four over and over. If you find your positive feelings waning, repeat step three before resuming with step four.

It can be a wonderful experience to feel gratitude for something you have yet to obtain. It's strange at first because most people feel a sense of lack when they don't have something. If you can accomplish this seemingly counterintuitive process, however, you may find many aspects of your life starting to line up with your goals.

Exercise #4: Vision Board

The vision board exercise is like the peanut butter to the chocolate of Audacious Visualization. What I mean to say is that they go together extremely well. The first step of this exercise is to go ahead and create your vision board. In the past, I imagine people clipped pictures out of newspapers and magazines and glued them to poster board. Nowadays, it's easy to create a specific vision board using an online image search and a free design program. Personally, I used this method to find my vision board's beach house picture, $100,000 bills picture and beautiful romantic dinner on an island picture. Pair this method with a color printer or a local printing center and you've got yourself a high-quality vision board.

The real trick, and the crux of this exercise, is to make looking at your vision board a part of your routine. One way to do this is to place it somewhere you always look, like near your desk or on the wall of your cubicle. No matter where you put it, it's important to set aside a bit of time to concentrate on it. You can put a $1,000 bill near your wallet, but unless you put it inside and actually spend it on something, it won't do you much good.

Once you've determined a location and a time, here is the method for using your vision board:

1. Focus on an image and imagine it as a part of your life. Be grateful and attempt to expand that positive feeling.
2. If any complimentary images come to mind, focus on them with the same grateful positivity.
3. Let go of the thoughts but keep the same joyful expectancy as you begin to look at the next image, repeating steps one and two.

During my senior year wrestling season, our motto was "Expect to Win." What a fantastic mindset to have. If you expect to lose, as many of us do in multiple parts of our lives, you will fulfill that prophecy. Expecting to win and expecting the images on your vision board to come true is what the Law of Attraction is all about.

It's possible that people who see you looking at a picture of the things you want in your life may make fun of you. This is another one of those cases in which, I'd rather be successful than cool. Several extremely wealthy and happy individuals in history have used the concept of the vision board to get them to the top. You may as well take some ribbing now as you slowly but surely climb that ladder to creative success.

Exercise #5: Mastermind

Sometimes, one or two heads just aren't enough. If you want to stretch the ideas that go into your creative projects, a mastermind is one of the most effective ways to accomplish this. The first step is to get together a group of at least three and as many as seven people who agree to meet at least once for a trial run. When choosing your motley mastermind crew, you want to make sure not to include anybody who could take over the meeting. This includes extremely type-A personalities who make everything about them, and this also includes friends who can't help talking about their social lives. Also, avoid including extremely negative individuals who would think such a meeting to be stupid or pointless and who would consider derailing the entire process for sport. Your best candidates for an effective mastermind are good listeners who have large goals and love giving advice or helping others.

Once you've got your crew together, have everyone spend a few minutes talking about their week through the lens of working on their purposeful goals. As suggestions come up for the speaker to take positive subsequent steps to the desired end result, she should write them down or take them to heart. I mean, how often do you have multiple minds working for you on typically internal concerns? Writing down potential tidbits of wisdom is key. After everybody has had a turn, using the help of the group, each person can determine steps for the following week. Even just two or three action steps can allow you to make major progress. Seeing an entire group make progress individually is quite a motivational feat to behold.

The real trick of a mastermind is to keep the group together (the same is true for bands). People get busy and it can be tough to get everyone together every time. Try your hardest to pick a time that each person can do for the foreseeable future and try to change on the fly if situations change. A mastermind is all about momentum, and if you can keep the group together for months or years, the amount of progress you can achieve together will make the happy fulfillment of your goals much more attainable. If many hands make light work, many brains make light and achievable goals.

The Plan

It's possible that this is my favorite set of exercises because it is the workout that would have most helped me when I first left college. While getting together a mastermind group may be difficult, the rest of these can be easily done at any time in the convenience of your own home. If you can't find like-minded folks for the group right away, don't fret; a few months of the other exercises will tend to make you gravitate toward folks that fit a mastermind quite nicely.

Monday: Begin the week by keeping your Physical Energy Journal

Tuesday: Pair the Vision Board with Audacious Visualization

Wednesday: Pump up hump day with a good night of Sleeping Beauty

Thursday: Repeat Tuesday

Friday: Take a look at the Physical Energy Journal and look for changes you can make.

Saturday and Sunday: Hold your Mastermind on the weekend or another day that works for the group.

Final Thoughts

Creativity is difficult to cultivate and valuable to employ, but it is unfortunately easy to discard because it can feel like a major burden. A creative life is not an easy one but it can be the most rewarding. Consider me a survivor of trying to lead such an existence who is telling you that it's possible. Don't give up on your dreams or waste your time. Learn how to turn your talents into a career and your desires into a reality. It seems like a precipitous mountain to climb at first, but true happiness waits on the other side.

CHAPTER 7: GOD AND HIGH SPIRITS

This is probably the part of the book that people are either going to love or hate. When I started brainstorming the idea for *The Post-College Guide to Happiness* several years ago, one of my first concerns was whether or not I should include God. While I'd seen other books about happiness touch on the subject, they typically take the kid gloves approach by talking about spirituality in vague terms or by trying to represent all viewpoints equally. Not everybody who reads this book will believe in God. Others who read it may believe in God but also think that firebombing clinics and killing innocent people are perfectly legitimate practices (which doesn't fly with this book).

My girlfriend and I have had long talks about how much religion is appropriate in a life and a family.

While both of us believe in God or a higher power, she wasn't brought up a particular religion, whereas I was brought up Jewish, had a bar mitzvah and went to evening Hebrew school. After college, I learned about different types of spirituality to incorporate into my life, such as the abundance mindset, which counteracts the belief held since the Dark Ages that piety should be connected with avoiding money like the plague (see what I did there?). While my girlfriend isn't convinced that she would want to raise a family with any hint of a particular religion, I believe that there are a lot of benefits to including religion and certain concepts of God in a family.

There are many negative parts of religion, of course, such as the hate and violence I've mentioned. I don't think that reading a short chapter in a book on happiness would be the kind of thing to turn around a person who has equated God with hating or ostracizing every person in the world who sees God in a different light. Here's what I am hoping by including what could be a controversial chapter: I believe that people who, during and after college, wear their religion like a thick, coat, trying to keep everything and everyone else who doesn't resemble them out may find themselves less happy then they ought to be. I would love it if someone reading this book realized that religion can be used to bring people of different beliefs together, not to separate them and not to single them out.

In addition, I feel that people who embrace religion and God should be open to leniencies in their beliefs that would allow for some amazing spiritual practices. I mentioned the Law of Attraction earlier. Many of those who have seen it work in their lives, as I have, do not see it as a pagan ritual or some kind of wacky cult. They see it as a unique type of prayer that doesn't start with "I'm sorry" but begins with "Thank you." This gratitude combined with picturing the life you want to have isn't about greed or not being worthy, it's about trusting in God as your supply. Now, I realize that some people reading this paragraph might go, "Oh, here Bryan comes, he was a religious freak all along." I will respond to this claim a bit later in the chapter.

Money is an important part of leading a happier life. Many religious folks think that wanting any sort of boost financially is somehow against God. In many instances in history, however, rich individuals have used their large earnings to contribute to worthwhile causes. Andrew Carnegie, who attributed his wealth to God, spent the last two decades of his life spending his money establishing public libraries (around 3,000 of them), universities (Carnegie Mellon University and the Tuskegee Institute) and even the spread of music to churches (7,000 organs). One could make the argument that God at least wanted Carnegie to become wealthy to support these many worthwhile causes. The first American billionaire, John D. Rockefeller, is attributed as saying "God gave me my money," spent his last four decades on philanthropy. Rockefeller tithed ten percent of his earnings to his church throughout his entire career, became one of the first benefactors of medical science, funding research that eradicated yellow fever and hookworm, and gave generously to the arts. Did God want Rockefeller to be poor as opposed to contributing those causes? These men weren't just rich. They used their riches appropriately to help others, a concept I'll talk about later in this chapter.

Is it more probable that God wants us to have everything we need or that some of us should struggle mightily? Writers like Catherine Ponder take a Prosperity Theology approach to biblical teachings and believe that these texts are more like handbooks to prosperity then reminders that we should live in standard to sub-standard conditions. According to Ponder, not only are we able to get what we need, but also some of the things we want that might make our lives more comfortable or productive.

Wealth doesn't mean much without having the health to enjoy it. There has always been a certain degree of fear when it comes to incorporating Eastern beliefs of spirituality with Western concepts of God. When I learned about the healing concepts of Eastern practices such as Qigong, I immediately attributed them to God. Using the idea that energy flows through the universe and can be used to not only heal yourself but to heal others around the world was something I had to try. Spring Forest Qigong practitioner Chun Yi Lin has the philosophy of "a healer in every family and a world without pain." If injury and illness has been a major part of your life and standard prayer has not had a lot of effect, I see it as perfectly logical to turn practices like Qigong into a sort of religious prayer for healing.

How to Pray Right

When we were children, many of us were unintentionally trained to whine and cry to get what we wanted. If we caused enough of a fuss, then we were bound to get that toy we wanted for our birthdays.

Perhaps that is one of the reasons why many of us tend to go about praying in the same way. We only think about something we need when we're in a state of despair and our shout to the heavens resembles, "Why have you forsaken me, Lord? I need to make my mortgage payment, please help." And then said shouter is surprised when his prayer goes unanswered. Interestingly enough, just like school doesn't teach us how to think, our religion doesn't teach us how to pray.

The best kind of prayer is the one that falls in line with the Law of Attraction. Such a prayer should have three components: gratitude, positivity and faith. The first part of a prayer should always begin with a "thank you." Even if you're in a rough spot right now, it wasn't always this way and it won't always be this way. Thank God or the universe for what you've had and what you have. Immediately you'll notice that this cuts through your negativity a considerable amount. That's the idea. For some reason, prayers that begin with negativity tend not to make it past the gatekeepers. Embrace the things you are thankful for and focus on the positivity associated with them. One way to send your prayer to new heights is to thank God for something extremely positive and joyful. The more positive your prayer's beginning, the more likely it is to be answered. Once you truly have the positive angle covered it's time to move on to having faith.

Now, you may be saying "Of course you have to have faith, that's the damn point." First of all, watch your mouth, there are twenty-somethings reading this book. Secondly, just like you need the right kind of prayer, you need the right kind of faith as well. In this instance, faith means that you already believe and trust that God has the thing or circumstance you want all lined up for you. Picture what you want as vividly as you can and try to feel the joy and love that will coming from having it in your life. As you concentrate on this joy from knowing it will come to pass, thank God or the universe again from changing around the world to bring this thing to come to you in due time, never questioning that it will be yours.

If you are used to praying and find that what you ask for frequently comes your way, there is no need to change your routine. If you find that your prayers have been coming up short, try out this method of gratitude, positivity and faith to see an improvement in your spiritual results.

Also, keep in mind that if your prayer wishes ill or harm on anybody, it violates the positivity precept and it likely to cause the prayer to fail. Let's keep prayer on the up and up, people.

Where Does Money Come From?

You might think that this question has a pretty obvious answer. Of course, money comes from your company, your boss, your spouse, your investments, etc., right? I mean, it's a bit disempowering to think that money is like a faucet that can simply be turned off if you lose a job or if an investment craps out, but what other way is there? Is there another way to look at money that would stop it from shutting off at a moment's notice? The answer to the last question, if you ask the author to *The Abundance Book*, John Randolph Price, is yes. Price would agree with you that it's disempowering to view your money as a source that can easily be turned off. But Price would disagree with you about what that source is. According to Price, the source of all money is God.

We work so hard to please our bosses and put in half of our lives doing difficult work to put food on the table for our families. When hard times come, we pray that our company keeps us employed, but are we praying for the right thing? After I graduated from college, I assumed that I would always struggle financially unless I become a top-tier short actor like Tom Cruise. And struggle I did, for half a decade, because I thought money came from a boss and my boss wasn't paying me squat. Upon a suggestion from Marci, I tried out John Randolph Price's prosperity plan, which taught me that we already have the potential to gain great wealth because according to Price, God wants us to. This went against the belief that I'd had that poor people are closer to God.

Now am I saying that God wants us to have 30 Ferraris and a mansion that could house the population of a small country? No. Am I saying that God wants us to be mindless consumers that have the ability to buy up every meaningless item we can lay our hands on? I'm not saying that either, because that would go against the gratitude and appreciation concepts from earlier in the book. Buying up everything you can find and being obsessed with it is like worshipping money. Worshipping the almighty dollar isn't what we're going for here. What I am saying is that God wants us to be able to pay the rent on time, to live in a home that our family can be comfortable in and to have money with which we can create jobs and donate to important causes.

I didn't really understand this last point until I combined the belief systems of two different authors: Ayn Rand, author of *Capitalism: The Unknown Ideal*, and Michael E. Gerber, who wrote *E-Myth Revisited*. Rand, most famous for *Atlas Shrugged*, puts forth her belief that capitalism is the first moral economic system because it allows people to actually move up the economic ladder. This is unlike economic systems in the past where if you were born a peon, you were stuck as a peon for life. In Gerber's *E-Myth*, he theorizes that one of the main reasons you create a business is to create a system that could lead to your business spreading to many locations and providing many people with jobs. For example, Starbucks was a system created by Howard Schultz that spread far and wide and has given jobs to hundreds of thousands of peoples.

Not everybody needs to believe that capitalism is a moral system and that you build up a business not just for yourself but to potentially provide many people with jobs, but if you believe that being poor is mandated by God, you may be less likely to take advantage of this arrangement. I'm not sure if I will be one of the people who creates a system to employ so many, but I believe that if I can make enough money to pay people who support my writing, such as editors, public relations professionals, cover designers, etc., this spreads the wealth to other creative people. As these creative people earn more money, they have more freedom to develop the next idea that might create more jobs.

I don't think God wants us to be rich. I think God wants us to help each other reach the point that more of us can bring our ideas into reality.

But prosperity isn't just about creating better lives for our family and jobs for others. I mean, look at Mother Theresa. She believed that God was the source of money better than most. If she was ever lacking, she would pray and God would provide. She wasn't poor and she didn't believe that it was pious to be poor. She simply had better things to do than worry about money, so she left it up to God. We should follow Mother Theresa's example and "pray right" for money. If we are grateful to God for the money that we already have and we are positive about the belief we will receive an abundant source of money in the future *and* if we have faith that it will come, then we are more likely to earn more than enough then if we simply suck up to our bosses. If God is all powerful and beneficent, why would he want us to be poor? He doesn't, and with faith directed in the proper way, we won't be.

Not Just Wealth But Health

If someone told you she had figured out a major secret that had helped her to improve her life dramatically, would you believe her? Say that it had to do with health and that the secret had been used to heal tumors, cure chronic pain and improve mental clarity. A religious person might believe it had to do with the power of prayer and that person wouldn't be completely off. That same religious person might write off the secret once he found out it was a pagan-sounding Eastern healing method called Qigong. I learned about Qigong from a DVD called Spring Forest Qigong, which was led by a master named Chun Yi Lin. Master Lin was also featured in Marci's book and has written several books of his own. Qigong involves the movement of energy through the body to remove blockages that have occurred to cause sickness or pain. These blockages can be in the form of chronic injuries, cancer and many other ailments, and Master Lin's method has been successful with many of them.

Now, what you might be saying is, "Bryan, I was willing to give you the benefit of the doubt on praying correctly. I'm even willing to give this 'Money comes from God' thing a shot. But ancient Eastern healing secrets? What does that even have to do with God?" Well, more than you might think.

Here's my opinion about God's relationship to the Law of Attraction, the abundance mindset, Qigong and a host of other practices and beliefs. If God exists and wants us to be happy, then he would probably leave us the tools to be happy, healthy and fiscally comfortable. But, He isn't necessarily going to make it easy or obvious for us to figure out what all those tools resemble. For instance, the Law of Attraction is a little bit Buddhist, while the abundance mindset has some roots in Judaism and Christianity and Qigong hails from Eastern beliefs of the body, energy and spirituality. Why wouldn't God make these different aspects of a happy life into a veritable jigsaw puzzle that needs to be deciphered? By doing things this way, God would allow people from different beliefs to come together and lead a good life in every conceivable way. Qigong focuses on energy coursing through the body; I might think of that energy as God. A Qigong practitioner might pray using the Law of Attraction and see it as energy and the universe bringing him what he wants.

You don't have to believe in God or a beneficent universe to be happy. But if you have a certain belief system, you don't have to use that belief to exclude yourself from being happy, either.

Meet You Halfway

When I discussed the Law of Attraction earlier, I mentioned how you have to meet the universe halfway, or you aren't likely to get what you want. Whatever you call it – prayer, the Law of Attraction, strange coincidence – you aren't likely to get the things you ask for in life unless you do some action on your own. One of my favorite quotes from the hilarious movie *Easy A* is uttered when an extremely religious student played by Amanda Bynes defends her boyfriend who has repeated senior year four times by saying, "If God wanted him to graduate high school, he would have given him the answers." We laugh and it's silly, but there are tons of people who leave their lives up to God without being willing to do things on their own.

One of my favorite illustrations of this is an old tale I first heard told by Earl Nightingale. A man is on the roof of his house because of a horrible flood that has risen to the second level of his house. A boatman passes by and says that he has enough room for the man in his vessel. The man says, "That's OK, God will save me from this flood." The boat leaves, the floodwaters rise, and the man drowns. When the man talks to God in heaven he asks, "God, why didn't you save me from that flood?" God replies, "Didn't you see the boat I sent you?"

If you keep your mind open to spirit, many synchronicities will seem to occur. Marci had to point this fact out in *Happy for No Reason* for me to start recognizing it. For me to get to the point of writing this book, I had to randomly stumble upon a personal development website, that helped me stumble upon a website creation tool, that arbitrarily gave me the keyword for writing prompts, that randomly led to my first book, that happened to sell well enough to let me quit my job and allow me to focus on this book. But maybe it wasn't so random. Before all of that happened, I prayed to God to help me out of this situation and to let me work on something that would leave me fulfilled. I had no idea what the path would be, but at any point if I had assumed any of these steps would just fall in my lap, I might never have reached the point I have today.

If you want to lead a more fulfilling and happier life and you learn about an interesting new project you can be a part of, give it a shot. If you meet a new person who seems to have a life closer to the one you want, strike up a friendship. If a family member brings up a cool idea you've never heard of, ask him more about it. In order to let God, the universe or spirituality give you a helping hand in your life's direction, take the signs that help is coming and meet them halfway.

Workout for God and High Spirits

Exercise #1: Giving Thanks

Praying in the most effective way possible can take some practice. One of the best ways to put in the praying reps at the spirituality gym is to start giving thanks as often as possible. Give yourself a challenge at the beginning of a particular wish to thank your higher power for something that you have or that you're going to have in the future at least 10 times in one day. I suggest writing this challenge down on a card or a post-it note that you'll see from time to time throughout your day. You may even want to start the day by listing 10 things to give thanks for and then check off each item as you do it. It's best to spread these throughout your day, since they act as little pick-me-ups each time you do it.

How you want to express your moments of thanks is up to you. You can write down a little note when something good happens. You can think a universal thank you to God for your secure career when work is getting you down. You can thank God out loud in the shower for the financial abundance that is coming your way and how you will use it to benefit others. However you want to do it, make sure there is no hint of sarcasm and that you aren't doing a "thanks, but..." followed by something negative. Be genuine, be grateful and be positive and your tiny moments of thanks throughout the day will make a big difference.

Exercise #2: Prosperous Mantra

Part of the reason that prayer works is rooted in the subconscious mind. If you thank God for a pony in your mind that you do not yet possess, not only does the universe begin to shift to a reality in which you have a pony, but deep down, your brain begins to figure out how to obtain said pony. Some people would argue it's all a matter of the brain pushing you in that direction subconsciously, while others would say that God did all the work. Since it's difficult to prove either way, I'm gonna go ahead and say both forces are at work. If that is the case and giving thanks helps God to know what you want, then it's up to us to optimize the subconscious mind part of the equation.

In Catherine Ponder's *The Divine Laws of Prosperity*, she discusses three methods for improving your chances of prosperity. She suggests that you write down what you're thankful for and what financial things you want in life. She recommends using a vision board (which I mentioned in the last chapter). Thirdly, she says that adding a spoken mantra to your routine can benefit you financially.

The mantra reads: "I am surrounded by divine substance. This substance now manifests for me in rich, appropriate form."

I realize that adding a mantra to this book makes it feel like it has devolved to the Stuart Smalley School of Self Help. This mantra, however, works as a bit of a subconscious wake-up call, rousing your faith and making you feel more confident that financial good times are headed your way.

I have used this mantra frequently since learning it. I have changed a word or two to make it less clunky and I suggest doing the same if you so desire. I truly believe that it has made an impact on the ideas I've come up with and the choices I've made, which have led to my increased financial success. Even if this is all a bunch of hooey, there is nothing wrong with adding to your optimism with such an internally stirring mantra. Optimistic people are by definition much happier, and if saying a wacko thing out loud about "divine substance" and being "rich" can add to those happiness levels *and* may coincidentally increase your income then you might as well go for it.

Exercise #3: Healing on the Go

There are lots of valuable exercises in Master Lin's Spring Forest Qigong products. I even once participated in his over-the-phone distance healing sessions, which were awesome. But not all of us have time to get into a semi-meditative state for an hour a day. Thankfully, Master Lin has developed a healing exercise for while you're on the go. It's an adaptation of his Breathing of the Universe exercise that you can use any time that you are walking (or sleeping or sitting, for that matter).

Here's how it works:

1. As you walk, unfold your arms and leave a little bit of space between your fingers to open up your energy channels. Breathe a few deep breaths and concentrate on the stillness of the universe.
2. State the phrase internally or verbally, "I am in the universe, the universe is in my body, the universe and I combine together."
3. Imagine energy flowing through your body and that any sickness or pain turns into butterflies and floats out of your body.
4. Internally state the phrase, "During this walk (or rest, etc.), all of my blockages turn into butterflies and exit my body."
5. Continue breathing and cycle back through the exercise until you feel as though the pain has abated. If you continue to think of the pain it will return, so focus instead on the quietness of the universe.

I can attest to feeling a powerful burst of energy when I feel that the blockages of pain and illness in my body have been removed. This isn't necessarily about reducing physical pain, either. The process can be used to work on your mental blocks as well. If you find yourself procrastinating or afraid to move forward on a particular project, Healing on the Go works well when paired with a cobwebs-clearing stroll. When I have mental baggage, Qigong is one of the first tools I turn to in order to regain a happy mental balance.

Exercise #4: Signing Off

When you begin to put together all of this happiness mumbo jumbo, you'll notice that a lot of synchronicities begin to happen. You will open yourself up to friendship with strangers and start to work on your passive income and all of a sudden, "Bam!" You'll meet the exactly the person you needed to help you take the next step forward. You'll send a positive thought someone's way as you think about your purpose and "Bam!" You see a magazine article with a new idea for a career direction (I don't know why these synchronicities make the Emeril "Bam!" sound, but just go with it). These events occur especially often when the Law of Attraction is involved. The trick with these seemingly random happenstances is that you have to be on the lookout for them.

Here are some examples of potential signs to look for:

- Meeting a new person who you seem to connect with almost immediately, who happens to be involved in your line of work.
- Receiving a random e-mail from a person who wants to collaborate or pick your brain.
- Multiple people telling you about the same job opening or other opportunity.
- A feeling that you should attend a particular event.
- An idea that keeps popping into your head that gives you a burst of energy.

Obviously, not everything that happens is some kind of destiny-laden sign that will guide you to changing the world (or the world changing you). But sometimes, you have to believe in everything as opposed to nothing, because you stand to gain a lot by listening to the universe every so often. During my trip to Israel a few years ago, always the storyteller, I got onto my tour bus microphone and told a wild tale from college. As the bus rumbled along in the desert and my trip-mates laughed at my ridiculousness, I had a feeling. The feeling was that half a world away, I should quit my coffee shop job because there was something out there better for me. Even though it was scary,

I decided to listen to this internal sign. Now here I am, telling some stories to all of you. I'm glad I listened.

Not all signs will be nearly as drastic or dramatic, so it's best to keep your eyes peeled and your ears open. Take at least a day during the week to practice looking for these signs and understanding the forms they might come in. Even if you decide to look out for them for only a short period of time, you'll be surprised to see how often they pop out when you're paying attention.

Exercise #5: Find the Beauty (Not the Fault)

We have a tendency to criticize the things that we don't truly understand. We'd rather relate these confusing foreign things to concepts that we already have a firm grasp upon than listen and learn about new ideas. This is especially true with religion. I've heard plenty of pointless back-and-forth arguments about particular passages in the Torah or Bible and between people from different religious backgrounds on the nature of God. Maybe this is why a weekly dinner party I used to attend instituted a rule of no religion and no politics (also no poultry, guess it wasn't the place for talking turkey). These conversations would be a lot different if, instead of arguing, these people learned to appreciate the beauty of each person's viewpoint.

When any being expresses a spiritual belief, it's like she's revealing a part of who she is. If you disagree with that viewpoint and argue your own belief vehemently, she will think that you are insulting her directly. This is why people can have such heated conflicts over religion. It's like telling a joke about someone's momma, except about 10 times more personal. It makes sense to take a different, less divisive, more inclusive approach.

Here is how to find the beauty in a conversation (not the fault):
1. Listen to a person talk about his religion or a particular belief.
2. Instead of responding with your own belief, respond in one of two ways.
    a. State how part of what he said is beautiful in a specific way without mentioning your religion.

116

      b. State how using said concept in his life might make him feel a certain way (cite a specific emotion you think the other person is feeling based on the way he said his belief to show that you are actually listening.)

3. Listen to his response. Repeat step two as the conversation continues.

4. Only respond with your belief system if you are asked. Keep in mind, being asked for your opinion doesn't necessarily mean responding with your beliefs.

Essentially, this is an application of classic empathic listening to a potentially contentious religious discourse. There is something wonderful about noticing the beauty in another person's religion. Finding something you appreciate in a different religion doesn't mean you don't believe in your version of God anymore, it just means that you're willing to connect with other people regardless of their faith. I realize that there are some religions that state a belief that people with other belief systems are going to hell. Look, you can believe what you want to believe, but stating this hellish belief is a conversation killer and an argument firecracker. If you hold such excluding beliefs, do your best to follow the above steps to connect with those of other faiths. I hope the exercise can lead to more love and happiness to go with your firmly established faith.

The Plan

For this workout plan, we've got a few things you could stand to do every day and a couple others that might only come up every so often. For instance, with Find the Beauty, you might need to seek out people of different faiths to converse with if you're isolated or in a cult.

Monday: Try Giving Thanks throughout the day along with an evening Prosperous Mantra

Tuesday: Test out Healing on the Go

Wednesday: Repeat Monday

Thursday: Keep your eyes peeled for Signing Off

Friday: Repeat Monday

Saturday and Sunday: When you come in contact with other faiths, try to Find the Beauty

Final Thoughts

I might have lost a few of you with this chapter. That's OK, I figured it was important enough to include even if it pissed off a few atheists and a handful of the more rigidly religious. If you are using your religion to sequester yourself and your family and you wonder why your prayers are going unanswered, I hope this chapter can help. God doesn't want you to be poor, unhealthy or isolated. A belief in spirituality is something you can use both for extreme gratitude and to create a successful life for yourself. A lot of religion is associated with guilt. I think it's time we changed that affiliation to one of happiness and fulfillment.

CHAPTER 8: A FULLY ROUNDED LIFE

Before I start into this chapter of bringing all of these seven sets of exercise full circle, I want to make sure everybody understands something. In no way am I saying that being in your head every once in a while and being cautious is going to make you unhappy. I don't want you to think that if you work in an office and you want to earn a lot of money will ensure that you don't find fulfillment. The same is true if you got married right out of college, if you plan on getting multiple degrees, if you play around on your phone every so often, if you have a creative dream but haven't been able to realize it yet or if you belong to a church, synagogue or mosque. What I am saying is that if you bury yourself in any one of those paths, which many people do as soon as they leave college, you need to step back and evaluate your life every so often. Maybe you're spending too much time on the computer and perhaps some of the beliefs at your current religious establishment are somewhat limiting. Life is like a stock portfolio. If you put all of your money toward one stock, you're completely dependent on it succeeding. All I'm suggesting is that you diversify your portfolio.

Now, it can be overwhelming to try to put all of this stuff together. This is one of the reasons that I formed the book as I did. While some people tend to fit into several of the seven chapters I laid out, I figured that most would relate most to one chapter, which would only give a few concepts and just five exercises to work on to increase their level of happiness. Some of us, however, may fit into nearly all of the categories at once. For you, I hope that the way the book is formatted doesn't scare you off, as if your happiness will be too difficult to achieve.

Truth be told, to lead a happier life doesn't mean working on all 35 exercises in this book every single day of your existence. I believe that by tweaking a few things you can lead a much more fulfilled life, saving yourself decades of potentially heading in the wrong direction (in the wrong jungle). If you were to focus on five aspects of the book to bring yourself up out of the muck of unhappiness, here are some good ones in no particular order.

1. Gratitude: It's possible that of all the ways happiness can be generated, this is one of the simplest and most underutilized methods. We have a holiday set up for family and friends to get together to show thanks, but in actuality, this practice should be a part of our daily ritual. Replacing your complaining and blaming with gratitude can make a huge amount of difference in no time at all.

2. Purpose: You have the ability to do some amazing stuff in this world. The chances of you accomplishing these goals are so much higher if you set up a grand purpose for yourself. Having a clear purpose in life puts a jump in your step and makes all of the work you do less difficult. Plus, if you don't come up with your own purpose, your brain makes one for you, which tends to involve shiny lights and hefty portions.

3. Connection: Learning to connect with the people you love, the friends who support you with positivity and those with different beliefs from your own can make a major impact on your life. It is possible to be an extremely independent person who has still forged amazing connections with others. Those connections can increase your chances of achieving goals, can lift you up when you're feeling down and can build up your levels of selfless happiness.

4. Thinking: If you can't think, you are unlikely to shake the fog of routine long enough to even know what would make you happy. Without spending some time on brainstorming it will be difficult for you to identify the areas of your life that could use sprucing up. The people who leave themselves time for

contemplation come up with the ideas that change the world. Choose thoughts over mindless routine.

5. Love: Love other people. Love yourself. Love the world around you. Happiness can't reach its highest potential without a dose of love. Even if you can warm your heart enough to love just one thing and one person, you will absolutely boost your levels of joy through the roof.

While everybody in the world deserves happiness, the truth of the matter is that happiness is earned and that it must be worked to reach its highest level possible. If you were a marathon runner and you stopped running for an entire year, would you expect your level of fitness and your effectiveness to improve? No, of course not. The same thing goes for happiness. Personally, every time I leave my bliss to the wind for a few months, I realize that no matter what time I gained by skipping my happiness exercises, I would pay for it later with undue malcontent. It can be irritating to know that, just like eating right and exercising properly, happiness depends on putting in the time and effort as well, but it's certainly better than having no control over the situation.

We like to consider ourselves helpless creatures. We say that the direction we've taken was out of our control; why else would we be at a job we dislike with friends that don't treat us as well as we deserve? The thing is, we are not powerless when it comes to choosing our own lives. Advances in the world have shown us that we can control our health through diet and exercise when we used to think it was completely up to chance. Through the concepts expressed in this book, now we know that we can control our thoughts and reactions, our levels of physical and emotional energy, how we spend our time, how we treat our loved ones and how to wield multiple streams of income. Happiness isn't about glittery toys or finding the perfectly sized and shaped partner. It's about enforcing your innate ability to control your own life. If you let yourself control your own life, you'll be happy. If you don't, you are leaving a heck of a lot up to chance.

We all have regrets in our lives and times that we've acted the opposite of the way we felt we should have. We tend to combine all these bad things that we've done into this part of ourselves that makes us feel like we don't truly deserve happiness. I'm here to tell you that you *do* deserve happiness and that everyone deserves a second chance to start fresh. People like to say that life is short. I'm going to go ahead and disagree. Life is long and you have the ability to lead many different lifetimes in your 80-plus-year span here. Start leading the one in which you actually enjoy your time. Don't go down a path that you've heard will lead to happiness, go down the one that you make for yourself. This is not a life for disappointment, jealousy and zoning out. Your life is one that is meant to be enjoyed, shared and fulfilled. While I would love the book sales, I don't care if it's my book that passes the message on. I want to live in a world where everybody who graduates from college or reaches a certain age finds out about the information here and can head, without stumbling, toward their own personal brands of happiness. Perhaps in an existence with constant innovation and development, that can be the next step to a better, happier planet.

APPENDIX 1: THE 35 EXERCISES SIMPLIFIED

I realize that we don't live in the most patient of worlds (please see Chapter Five) and that some of you might want to simply cut to the chase and start working on increasing your happiness levels. While I think that what I've said in between the action steps in the earlier chapters has been important (or I wouldn't have written it), I have decided to include this section, which is just the exercises and a one sentence description for each. To get a full sense of what each exercise has to offer, go back to the end of the chapter the exercise is from. While the exercises are geared to certain aspects of happiness, any of the 35 exercises can boost your overall level of joy, no matter what you do and who you are.

Brainy Bliss

1. Mental Aerobics – Try activities your brain isn't used to so that you can stimulate the right chemicals needed to change your mind for the better.

2. I Spy – Appreciation Edition – Look for things in the world to appreciate to boost your mood.

3. The Sedona Method® – Realize that by asking yourself if you want to keep certain feelings that they aren't attached to you and are easy to let go of.

4. Optimism Journal – Keep track of the way you respond to adversity with your beliefs so that you can try new tactics that lead to different consequences.

5. A New Project – To stimulate your brain and improve your feelings of accomplishment, take on a new project in your life.

Money and Happiness

1. Rewrite Your Goals – Rewrite your goals by hand every morning to impress them into your subconscious.

2. Enthusiasm – Force yourself to be enthusiastic at work for a short period of time and see how it transforms your life and your emotions.

3. The Eulogy – Write down an account of how you want to be remembered at the end and then live that life instead of the one you're living.

4. Talking Purpose – Get some positive friends together and talk about the direction of your life to generate new ideas and feel validated.

5. Passive Income – Generate a source of income that works for you while you're sleeping.

True Love and Contentment

1. The Mirror Exercise – Look at yourself, find the good things, and tell yourself about them.

2. Solutions Focus – Tell your partner all the wonderful reasons you two are not a "1" and focus on them.

3. Proofs of Love – Find little and big ways to show your partner that you care.

4. Gratitude List – Come up with a collection of things you are happy for in your lives together to boost your positivity and appreciation.

5. The Highlight Reel – Gather your family together to talk about positive memories and then express them artistically to make them stick out.

Education and Joy

1. My Philosophy – Come up with your own way of thinking that isn't tainted by the perspective of others to validate yourself.

2. Twenty Minutes for Me – Take time off of academia and employment to do something for nobody but yourself.

3. Self-Disaster Kit – Create a list of the things that you have to offer independent of degrees and education and brainstorm ways that you can use your "acres of diamonds."

4. Thinking Improvement – Set aside some time to think completely for yourself and to figure out ways that you can improve your life.

5. Network Coverage – Go outside your academic circle to talk to other people and find out how what you're doing may be able to benefit them.

Gratification and Peace

1. Just Stand There – Test your patience by not touching any electronic devices and simply standing there for a short period of time.

2. Subconscious Text Messages – Relax and meditate your way deep inside to collect your own internal text message that may help you to lead a more connected life.

3. Seven Loving Thoughts – Send a series of loving thoughts to strangers and acquaintances you pass by throughout the day.

4. A Night in the Past – Disconnect all of your electronics for the night and live a night in the past by directly connecting with your loved ones.

5. The Informed Statement – A little listening to the people you meet and a tiny informed statement can go a long way to connecting with them on a deeper level.

Creativity and Lifelong Dreams

1. Physical Energy Journal – Keep track of your energy boosts and drains throughout the day to learn the ways you can increase your stores of physical energy.

2. Sleeping Beauty – Keep yourself away from stimulants and go to bed early.

3. Audacious Visualization – Visualize yourself getting amazing and wonderful things that you want in this world with an extremely positive mindset.

4. Vision Board – Create a collage of the wonderful things you want to be a part of your life while keeping an extremely positive mindset.

5. Mastermind – Meet with a group of uplifting people regularly to discuss ways that you can improve the accomplishment of your goals.

God and High Spirits

1. Giving Thanks – Thank the universe for the things that you have in your life and maybe a few things that you want to have that you have faith will come your way.

2. Prosperous Mantra – State out loud that you believe that universe will provide for you and that riches are headed to you because you believe.

3. Healing on the Go – Using Eastern healing methods mixed with your Western beliefs, send energy to relieve the pain and sickness in your body to improve your health on the go.

4. Signing Off – Look for signs in your day-to-day life that might be pointing you in a particular direction to best achieve your goals.

5. Find the Beauty (Not the Fault) – Instead of arguing with people of other faiths, use empathic listening and gratitude to hold a positive conversation of appreciation.

APPENDIX 2: HAPPY PASSIVE INCOME

In Chapter Two, one of the exercises I presented is the creation of a new source of passive income in your life. I'm going to try to make that exercise easier on you by inviting you to join my affiliate program for this very book. The program consists of creating a page on my website and giving away free copies of the book to friends and acquaintances who you think might like it enough to write about it. I hope that by providing this program, I am able to both spread the word of the book and provide several hundred people with an added source of income that works for them 24 hours a day. To inquire about joining the program, send an e-mail to postcollegehappiness@gmail.com.

BIBLIOGRAPHY

Bettger, Frank (1992) *How I Raised Myself from Failure to Success in Selling*, New York: Fireside

Butler-Bowdon, Tom (2004) *50 Success Classics: Winning Wisdom for Work and Life from 50 Landmark Books*, London: Nicholas Brealey Publishing

Byrne, Rhonda (2006) *The Secret*, New York: Atria Books

Carlson, Richard (1997) *Don't Sweat the Small Stuff...and it's all small stuff: Simple Ways to Keep the Little Things from Taking Over Your Life*, New York: Hyperion

Conwell, Russell (1921) *Acres of Diamonds*, Marina del Rey, CA: DeVorss & Co.

Covey, Stephen (1989) *The 7 Habits of Highly Effective People*, London: Simon & Schuster

Dell, Michael with Catherine Fredman (1999) *Direct from Dell: Strategies that Revolutionized an Industry*, London: HarperBusiness

Doidge, Norman (2007) *The Brain That Changes Itself: Stories of Personal Triumph from the Frontiers of Brain Science*, New York: Penguin Group

Dwoskin, Hale (2007) *The Sedona Method : Your Key to Lasting Happiness*, Sedona: Sedona Press

Ford, Henry (1996) *My Life and Work*, Manchester, NH: Ayer Co. Publishing

Frankl, Viktor (1959) *Man's Search for Meaning*, Boston: Beacon Press

Gerber, Michael (1995) *The E-Myth Revisited: Why Most Small Businesses Don't Work and What to Do About It*, New York: HarperBusiness

Hicks, Esther and Jerry Hicks (2004) *Ask and It Is Given : Learning to Manifest Your Desires*, Carlsbad: Hay House, Inc.

Hill, Napoleon (1960) *Think and Grow Rich*, New York: Fawcett Crest

Hopkins, Tom (1993) *The Official Guide to Success*, W. Jamison (ed.), London: HarperCollins

Jackson, Paul Z. and Mark McKergoe (2007) *The Solutions Focus: Making Coaching and Change S.I.M.P.L.E.* London: Nicholas Brealey International

Katz, Lawrence & Rubin Manning (1999) *Keep Your Brain Alive : 83 Neurobic Exercises To Help Prevent Memory Loss and Increase Mental Fitness* New York: Workman Publishing Company, Inc.

Lin, Chun Yi (2000) *Spring Forest Qigong*, Minnetonka, MN: Learning Strategies Corporation

Loehr, Jim and Tony Schwartz (2003) *The Power of Full Engagement*, London: Nicholas Brealey Publishing

Nightingale, Earl (2002) *Lead the Field* New York: Simon & Shuster Audio

Pavlina, Steve (2011) *Personal Development for Smart People*, Available at http://www.stevepavlina.com

Ponder, Catherine (1962) *The Dynamic Laws of Prosperity*, Camarillo, CA: DeVorss & Co.

Price, John Randolph (1996) *The Abundance Book*, London: Hay House

Rand, Ayn (1967) *Capitalism: The Unknown Ideal*, New York: Signet

Robbins, Anthony (1986) *Unlimited Power: The New Science of Personal Achievement*, London: Simon & Schuster

Robbins, Anthony (1991) *Awaken the Giant Within : How to Take Immediate Control of Your Mental, Emotional, Physical & Financial Destiny!*, New York: Simon & Schuster

Rohn, Jim (1996) *7 Strategies for Wealth & Happiness: Power Ideas from America's Foremost Business Philosopher*, Roseville, Calif.: Prima Publishing

Rubin, Gretchen (2009) *The Happiness Project: Or, Why I Spent a Year Trying to Sing in the Morning, Clean My Closets, Fight Right, Read Aristotle, and Generally Have More Fun*, New York: HarperCollins Publishers

Seligman, Martin E.P. (1991) *Learned Optimism*, New York: A. A. Knopf

Shimoff, Marci with Kline, Carol (2008) *Happy For No Reason : Seven Steps To Being Happy from the Inside Out*, New York: Simon & Schuster, Inc.

Tracy, Brian (1993) *Maximum Achievement: Strategies and Skills that Will Unlock Your Hidden Powers to Succeed*, New York: Fireside

Tracy, Brian, (2010) *Goals! How to Get Everything You Want – Faster Than You Ever Thought Possible*, San Francisco: Berrett-Koehler Publishers, Inc.

Yunus, Muhammad (1999) *Banker to the Poor: The Autobiography of Muhammad Yunus, Founder of the Grameen Bank*, London: Aurum Press

Ziglar, Zig (2000) *See You at the Top: 25th Anniversary Edition*, Gretna, LA: Pelican Publishing

ABOUT THE AUTHOR

Bryan Cohen is an author, blogger, freelance writer, comedian and actor who is originally from Dresher, Pennsylvania. He has published seven books and plays including *1,000 Creative Writing Prompts: Ideas for Blogs, Scripts, Stories and More*; *Writer on the Side: How to Write Your Job Around Your 9 to 5 Job*; and *Chekhov Kegstand*. His website, Build Creative Writing Ideas (which can be found at http://www.build-creative-writing-ideas.com), serves over 15,000 visitors a month looking for creative inspiration. His writing services are available for hire at http://www.BryanCohen.com. He lives with his girlfriend in Chicago, Illinois.

Made in the USA
Coppell, TX
17 May 2021

55845112R10085